AMERICAN
PHILOSOPHY
TODAY
And Other
Philosophical Studies

AMERICAN PHILOSOPHY TODAY

And Other Philosophical Studies

Nicholas Rescher

Rowman & Littlefield Publishers, Inc.

ROWMAN & LITTLEFIELD PUBLISHERS, INC.

Published in the United States of America
by Rowman & Littlefield Publishers, Inc.
4720 Boston Way, Lanham, Maryland 20706

3 Henrietta Street, London WC2E 8LU, England

Chapter 1, "American Philosophy Today" was originally published
in *The Review of Metaphysics,* vol. 46, pp. 717-45. © 1993, *The Review
of Metaphysics.* Reprinted with permission.
Chapter 5, "Morality and the Military" was originally published as
"The Complexity of Military Obligation" by the U.S. Air Force Academy
in its Reich Memorial Lecture Series. Reprinted with permission.
Chapter 6, "Moral Obligation and the Refugee" was originally published
in *Philosophical Problems of the Internal and External Worlds,* edited by John
Earman, et. al., © 1994, University of Pittsburgh. Reprinted with permission.

British Cataloging in Publication Information Available

Library of Congress Cataloging-in-Publication Data

Rescher, Nicholas.
American philosophy today and other philosophical studies /
Nicholas Rescher.
p. cm.
Includes index.
1. Philosophy, Aemrican—20th century.   2. Ethics.   3. Philosophy.
I. Title.   II. Title: American philosophy today.
B945.R454R37 1994 191—dc20 94–16451 CIP

ISBN 0–8476–7935–7 (cloth : alk. paper)
ISBN 0–8476–7936–5 (pbk. : alk. paper)

Printed in the United States of America

FOR

VICTOR RODRÍGUEZ

IN CORDIAL FRIENDSHIP

CONTENTS

PREFACE

This volume is a collection of philosophical studies written over the past two years. Several of them have appeared in print in various journals and the details have in each case been given in the chapter's final endnote. I am grateful to the editors involved for reprinting permission. I am also grateful to Marian Kowatch for her patient help in word processing my hen-scratches.

Nicholas Rescher
Pittsburgh, Pennsylvania
April 1993

INTRODUCTION

THE ten studies collected together here are united by a methodological rather than a thematic unity. For although they traverse a rather diversified philosophical terrain, they are designed to exhibit a common *modus operandi*, deploying the clarificatory techniques that characterize the analytical tradition in the interests of elucidating some larger-scale issues of traditional concern in philosophy.

The philosophical mode of the present century differs from that of the past in one important respect. In the past there was a wall separating philosophical scholarship from philosophizing as such. This is a barrier that is now long fallen. With many recent writers concern for the history of philosophy and for the practice of philosophizing time became part of our seamless web. This general phenomenon is often exhibited in my own work—quite prominently so in some of the essays in the present volume.

More than any other creative intellectual discipline, philosophy has a special relationship to its past. The aim of philosophizing, to be sure, is not one of syncretism, of preserving and restructuring the tradition for its own sake. But it can always draw enormous profit for the work at hand by exploiting the ideas and arguments and visions of the tradition as a storehouse of tools for the accomplishment of these present labors. The basic issues of philosophy are perennial and crop up in a renewed, reacclimated guise in every era. And attention to the ways our predecessors have dealt with them is a resource of inestimable value in the accomplishment of our own work.

From the angle of the philosopher, there is nothing antiquarian about interest in the history of the subject. Indeed, it is highly profitable to look at the situation of the present in a "historical perspective"—to look inward at the work that we and our contemporaries are doing in the sort of way that we can plausibly expect (or hope) that historians of philosophy will do in days to come. This distancing from the present situation as we confront it can carry constructive lessons eminently useful to us in the context of our philosophical endeavors.

The studies presented here fall into three groups. The first deals with the present situation in philosophy and how matters have arrived there. The second examines some concrete issues in moral philosophy. And the third offers critiques of several currently influential philosophical positions. Taken together, the studies thus illustrate the historical, the systematic, and the critical modes of philosophizing. They exhibit the conjointly clarificatory and evaluative concern that not only characterizes their author's own philosophical style but is also typical of much of present-day philosophizing as well.

Chapter One

AMERICAN PHILOSOPHY TODAY

PERHAPS the most striking feature of professional philosophy in North America at this historic juncture (1992) is in scope and scale.[1] The historian Bruce Kuklik entitled his informative study of academic philosophy in the U.S., *The Rise of American Philosophy: 1860-1930*, even though his book dealt only with the Department of Philosophy of Harvard University.[2] This institution's prominence on the American philosophical scene in the early years of the century was such that this parochial-seeming narrowing of focus to one single department—with its half-dozen or so philosophers—was not totally absurd for the period at issue. But today it would certainly be so. The American Philosophical Association, to which most U.S. academic practitioners of the discipline belong, presently has almost 9,000 members (see Appendix 1, p. 23), and the comprehensive *Directory of American Philosophers* for 1992-93 lists well over 10,000 philosophers affiliated to colleges and universities in the U.S. and Canada.[3] Admittedly, this profession is small potatoes compared with other academic enterprises; the Scientific Research Society *Sigma Xi* currently has a membership of more than 100,000 scientists, the Modern Language Association has more than 32,000 members. All the same, a small town of not inconsiderable size could be populated exclusively with contemporary North American academic philosophers. To be sure, its demographics would be rather unusual. Only just under twenty percent would be women, and blacks, Hispanics, and Asian-Americans would (each) constitute just over one percent of the population. And its political orientation is decidedly liberal and capital-D Democratic. (Yet however much it may annoy the liberals among us, the fact is that the condition of the American philosophy professorate is still very much a matter of live white males teaching about dead ones.[4]) The social classes above and below the middle are underrepresented in this community, and a disproportionate fraction of its members come from families of professional status. Moreover, for reasons that require a deeper sociological analysis than can be attempted here, the profession attracts a disproportionately larger fraction of Catholics (generally practicing ones), of Jews (generally nonpracticing ones), and of immigrants. In general, American philosophers of the present era in general do not come from home backgrounds where the high matters of literacy or artistic interests played a significant role, and their own intellectual formation is more often that of an academic technician than that of an intellectual of the traditional European type.[5]

In an academic discipline of American philosophy's present size, two different—and sometimes opposed—tendencies are at work to create a balance of countervailing forces. The one is an impetus to separateness and differentiation—the desire of individual philosophers to "do their own thing," to have projects of their own and not be engaged in working on just the same issues as everyone else. The other is an impetus to togetherness—the desire of philosophers to find companions, to be able to interact with others who share their interest to the extent of providing them with conversation partners and with a readership of intellectual cogeners. The first, centrifugal tendency means that philosophers will fan out across the entire reach of the field—that most or all of the "ecological niches" within the problem-domain will be occupied.[6] The second, centripetal tendency means that most or all of these problem-subdomains will be multiply populated—that groups or networks of kindred spirits will form so that the community as a whole will be made up of subcommunities united by common *interests* (more prominently than by common opinions), with each group divided from the rest by different priorities as to what "the really interesting and important issues" are. Accordingly, the most striking aspect of contemporary American philosophy is its fragmentation. The scale and complexity of the enterprise is such that if one seeks in contemporary American philosophy for a consensus on the problem agenda, let alone for agreement on the substantive issues, then one is predestined to look in vain. Here theory diversity and doctrinal dissonance are the order of the day, and the only interconnection is that of geographic proximity.[7] Such unity as American philosophy affords is that of an academic industry, not that of a single doctrinal orientation or school. Every doctrine, every theory, every approach finds its devotees somewhere within the overall community.[8] On most of the larger issues there are no significant majorities. To be sure, some uniformities are apparent at the localized level. (In the San Francisco Bay area one's philosophical discussions might well draw on model theory, in Princeton possible worlds would be bought in, in Pittsburgh, pragmatic themes would be prominent, and so on.) But in matters of method and doctrine there is a proliferation of schools and tendencies, and there are few if any all-pervasively dominant trends. Balkanization reigns supreme.

The centrifugal tendencies are, however, in a way counterbalanced by centripetal ones. North American philosophers appear to be exceedingly gregarious by standards prevailing anywhere else. Apart from the massive American Philosophical Association, there presently exist some 120 different philosophical societies in the U.S. and Canada,[9] twenty-three of which claim over 500 members. In the main, these societies are of three types: subdisciplinary (for example, Metaphysical Society of America, Philosophy of Science Association), geographic (for example, Minnesota Philosophical Society, Virginia Philosophical Association), and person-oriented (for example, Leibniz Society of North America, C. S. Peirce Society). These societies provide the lifeblood of interpersonal interaction among American philosophers. Their aggregate effect is a vast network of meetings and conferences that keep colleagues of common interest in ongoing interaction with one another. Even the most energetic and affluent of persons would find it next to impossible to attend all the professional conferences and symposia that would be of interest to an even modestly versatile philosopher.[10] Some of the bigger of these societies adhere to large international bodies such as FISP (the International Federation of Philosophical Societies) or IUHPS (the International Union of History and Philosophy of Science). However, the activities of these UNESCO-sponsored umbrella organizations have little impact on American philosophers and none on American philosophy.

Outside the instructional context, philosophy also plays some role in various research centers that are affiliated to major universities, such as the National Humanities Center in the Research Triangle of North Carolina, the Center for Values and Social Policy at the University of Colorado, and the Center for Philosophy of Science at the University of Pittsburgh. Apart from colleges and universities, American philosophy gets a (very modest) slice of the academic research support pie through such U.S. federal programs as the National Endowment for the Humanities and the National Science Foundation. Moreover such privately funded providers of research support as the Guggenheim Fellowship Program or the MacArthur Foundation's "Creative Genius" Program also on occasion support the work of philosophers. In North America, philosophy is securely entrenched in the academic scheme of things. Nevertheless, the share of philosophy-and-religion is less than two percent of the college book market in the U.S., less than one quarter of that of psychology.[11] (In America, Freud and Co. have clearly won a signal cultural victory.)

One feature that distinguishes present-day activity in American academic philosophy from the situation at any earlier stage is the rise of historical studies. For in North America, research in the history of philosophy is currently in a remarkably active and flourishing state. Several hundred specialized books are published in this area each year—many of them of a level of technical expertise rarely attained in American contributions of an earlier era. There exist some dozen specialist journals in the field (including *Ancient Philosophy, Medieval Studies, Hume Studies, History of Philosophy Quarterly,* and *Journal of the History of Philosophy,* among others). And there are also some dozen specialist societies, most of them dedicated to the work and thought of a single great thinker of former times, including Leibniz, Hume, Hegel, Kant, Kirkegaard, Nietzsche, Whitehead, and Santayana. One third of American philosophy Ph.D. theses produced these days relate to historical issues.

It is, of course, possible and indeed necessary to distinguish between philosophers and philosophy professors—between those who are active contributors to the intellectual resources of the discipline and those who provide academic instruction in the field. But the fact is that in recent years the latter have largely become incorporated into the former group—that a growing professionalism based on more rigorous formal training and a "publish or perish" ethics in the academy has meant that the teaching staffs in American colleges are increasingly populated by people who are productive philosophers. For the fact is that American philosophers are quite productive. They publish well over 200 books per annum nowadays. And issue by issue they fill up the pages of over 175 journals.[12] Given that almost 4,000 philosophical publications (books or articles) appear annually in North America, and a roughly similar number of symposium papers conference presentations and the like, the line between teaching and substantive contribution is anything but hard and fast. To be sure, the aggregate published output of philosophers—some 120,000 pages per annum—does not match that of other branches of the academic profession. (In 1987 alone, American scholars in English literature published 544 articles on William Shakespeare, 215 on John Milton, and 132 on Henry James.[13]) But even without such scholarly overkill, the productivity of American philosophy is an impressive phenomenon—though one could certainly debate the quality of this production. (This is not due to defective skill—the technical ability of philosophers seems better than ever—but rather to a penchant for concentrating on philosophically peripheral, nay often trivial issues whose main attraction is that they also preoccupy other philosophers.)

Marshall McLuhan to the contrary notwithstanding, the book is still the key artifact of philosophizing. It continues to make a major impact, with works like W. V. Quine's *Word and Object*, Thomas Kuhn's *Structure of Scientific Revolutions*, John Rawls' *Theory of Justice*, and Richard Rorty's *Philosophy and the Mirror of Nature* casting large ripples across the pond. Nevertheless, even monographic books are declining in import, with collections of a particular author's essays or lectures often exerting an influence no less substantial. (Donald Davidson's *Essays on Actions and Events* and Saul Kripke's *Wittenstein on Rules and Private Languages* are illustrations of this phenomenon.) And in the background looms the fact that the vast diffuse journal literature is a formative force in present-day American philosophizing just as potent as the domain of books.

What is distinctive in American philosophy today is less a matter of *product* than one of *process*. For it seems appropriate to characterize contemporary American philosophy as a substantial *industry*—with thousands of operatives, many hundreds of worksites (college departments), scores of training institutes (universities), and a prolific and diversified range of products, including not only classes but books, journals, congresses, conferences. Throughout, a high degree of scholarly competency and professionalism pervades the enterprise. Considering the quantity of philosophical writing that sees the light of print, its overall quality is respectably high—at any rate if one's standard gives weight to the technical dimension. (Depth of insight is another matter.) At any rate, the day of the philosopher as isolated thinker—the talented amateur with an idiosyncratic message—is effectively gone. (For better or for worse, an outsider along the lines of a Spinoza or a Nietzsche would find it near to impossible to get a hearing in the North American philosophical world of today.)

The recent statistics of philosophy doctorates bring some interesting facts to light. (See Appendix 2.) The total number of doctorates awarded by institution of higher learning in the U.S. has been relatively stable at around 100,000 over the last years (101,000 for 1970-75 and 98,700 for 1980-85). But the production of philosophy doctorates has declined substantially (along with that of humanities Ph.D.s in general), seeing a 40 percent reduction from 1,178 for the former period to 746 for the latter. The proportionally increasing prominence of women among the new philosophy Ph.D.s (growing from 158 or 13 percent of the total for 1970-75 to 161 or 22 percent of the total for 1980-85) is a noteworthy phenomenon. But whatever victory this percentage gain represents for women seems a Pyrrhic one, seeing that they are in process of securing a somewhat larger share of a profession that is declining probably in status and certainly in economic terms. (In the American context those factors are seldom far apart.)

Employment opportunities within the philosophy industry are reasonably good for those who meet its elaborate entrance qualifications. In the later 1980s some 550 to 600 philosophy teaching posts were advertised annually in the U.S., with some 850 job seekers in pursuit of them. (Given that job seekers include people who already hold jobs but wish to change them, this would indicate that the profession is currently able to provide the great majority of its qualified practitioners with jobs.) As regards remuneration, the position of philosophers is typical of that of humanists in higher education. In the early 1990s beginning assistant professors of philosophy averaged some $28,000 per annum. Full professors of philosophy in U.S. colleges and universities currently have average annual salaries of some $58,000, which compares with $70,000 for professors of engineering and $84,000 for law professors.[14] (Professors of medicine, of course, are in quite another league.) Moreover, professors in general find themselves in an economically declining situation, with average salaries diminishing in real terms by over twenty percent from 1970 to 1990. It is ironic that in a period when the real cost of higher education has risen dramatically, the average real pay of those who staff the activity has declined dramatically. (The reason lies in the fact that the size of the professorate has expanded faster than that of its undergraduate clientele, with a negative impact on professional pay and status. See Appendix 1.)

The growth of the profession, the massification of the system of higher education, and the eroding economic status of the professorate all combine to make philosophy less of an elite endeavor than it used to be. This decline in elitism in American philosophy is illustrated in a graphic way when one considers the production of Ph.D.s in the departments of high-prestige universities. (See Appendix 3.) Of the five traditional "ivy league" institutions (Yale, Harvard, Princeton, Columbia, and the University of Pennsylvania) only Columbia currently figures on the roster of North American philosophy departments most productive of Ph.D.s. From the standpoint of Ph.D. training, the most prominent contribution is made by the big U.S. state universities (Michigan, Minnesota, New York, Texas, and Wisconsin) and by the large Catholic institutions. However, the biggest single producer of philosophy Ph.D.s in North America is the University of Toronto. The main shortcoming of our flourishing *system* of higher education in philosophy lies in its very nature as such, which accentuates quantity over quality. Graduate programs are in general not inclined to judge competence by technical skill applied to minutiae rather than demanding actual contributions to the subject as such. As military academies produce managers rather than warriors, so philosophy programs produce problem solvers rather than philosophers.

The very size of the academic industry is intimidating and engenders humility. For the individual professional confronts the sobering thought: Consider a thought experiment. Excise from American philosophy everything that is near and dear to you—every author and book and journal you actually read, every lecture you go to hear, every colleague you interact with. The result is still a large and thriving enterprise that has a healthy and active life of its own, irrespective of such an excision. The amputation would make a difference, but nowise a fatal one. The process as a whole would proceed much as before.

The size and scope of the academic establishment exerts a crucial formative influence on the nature of contemporary American philosophy. In the philosophical environment of the past, the role of the great figures was more prominent, and the writings of philosophers established a balance of indebtedness to "big names" as against "modest contributors" that was much more favorable to the former category than is the case today, when philosophical writers who make use of "the literature" are destined to take far more notice of the smaller fry simply because there are so many more of them.[15] In the past, the philosophical situation of academically developed countries could be described by indicating a few giants whose work towered over the philosophical landscape like a great mountain range, and whose issues and discussion defined the agenda of the philosophizing of their place and time. Once upon a time, the philosophical stage was dominated by a small handful of greats. Consider German philosophy in the nineteenth century, for example. Here the philosophical scene, like the country itself, was an aggregate of principalities—presided over by such ruling figures as Kant, Fichte, Hegel, Schelling, Schopenhauer, and a score of other philosophical princelings. But in North America, this "heroic age" of philosophy is now a thing of the past. The extent to which professionally solid and significant work is currently produced by academics outside the high-visibility limelight is not sufficiently recognized. The fact that in philosophical teaching, the topical anthology has in recent years gained a position of equality with if not dominance over the monographic philosophical text or treatise is just one illustration of this phenomenon.

Until around 1914, it was religion that exerted the dominant influence on philosophers writing in America. During the 1914-1960 era natural science served as the prime source of inspiration. But over the past generation the sources of inspiration have become greatly diversified. The stimulating essay by Richard Rorty on "Philosophy in America Today" (in *Consequences of Pragmatism* [Minneapolis, 1982], pp. 211-30) both describes and celebrates the postwar era's shift from a scientific model of philosophizing to a political model where "literary culture" is what matters most, and people proceed in "the sense that nature and scientific truth are largely beside the point and that history is up for grabs" (pp. 228-29). But this tendentious account envisions an unrealistic uniformity. The fact is that at present philosophy is a garden where 100 flowers bloom. In recent years the source of influence has fragmented across the whole academic board. Some look for inspiration to psychology (especially to Freud), others to economics (from Marx to von Neumann), yet others to literature, or to law, or to.... The list goes on and on. Contemporary American philosophy does not have the form of a histogram with a few major trends; it is a complex mosaic of many different and competing approaches.

Prominent examples of currently fashionable approaches are found in certain programmatic tendencies:

- to explicate the meaning of certain philosophical concepts by means of "truth" conditions—for example, free agency, or linguistic understanding,

- to explain human capacities (e.g., for knowledge or for understanding) in terms of models or analogies from computing machines and "artificial intelligence" considerations,

- to explain human rule-following practice in terms of social policies and norms,

- to explain human capacities (e.g., for knowledge or for understanding) on the basis of evolutionary theories and Darwinian natural selection.

Each such program sets the stage for a diversified multi-participant effect—a little "cottage industry" as it were. Often as not, they result from the provocation of some individual's or school's exaggerated claim along some such lines as that "all evaluations simply express people's attitudes" or "communicatively significant features of human linguistic performances root entirely in social norms."

For better or for worse, we have entered into a new philosophical era where what counts is not just a dominant elite but a vast host of lesser mortals. Principalities are thus notable in their absence, and the scene is more like that of medieval Europe—a collection of baronies. Scattered here and there in separated castles, a prominent individual gains a local following of loyal friends or enemies. But no one among the academic philosophers of today manages to impose their agenda on more than a minimal fraction of the larger, internally diversified community. Even the most influential of contemporary American philosophers is simply yet another—somewhat larger—fish in a very populous sea.

Appendix 4 gives some citation statistics for members of the American philosophy professorate of the present day. It is interesting to note that (as this appendix indicates) even on their home ground only a few of these American academics exert anything like as much influence within the profession as do various of their European contemporaries. Derrida, Habermas, and Ricoeur all easily outplay all of the home team when it comes to the scoring of citation indices (though, to be sure, those Appendix 4 figures reflect the situation not in philosophy alone, but also in the allied humanities). However different a situation may prevail in other areas like science or mathematics or economics, in philosophy many American professors continue to look to Europe for role models and for inspiration to a degree that would doubtless annoy Ralph Waldo Emerson who looked for a declaration of intellectual independence to succeed the political one. American philosophy is strikingly open to influences from abroad. With ideas as with consumer goods, Americans are eager to import while European philosophy is generally eager to enter the export business. (Which is not to say that a marked provincialism is not at work in other regards: In America, as elsewhere, domestic stars of the third magnitude are far more likely to have their work noted by fellow countrymen than foreign stars of the second.)

If one looks to such currently widespread ideological tendencies of American philosophy as analytic philosophy, neo-positivism, Wittgensteineanism, hermeneutics, and Heideggerianism, and the like, then one notes that virtually all of them—neo-pragmatism apart—have roots in European thinkers. (Europe, after all, is the home of ideologies.) But much of American philosophy—like much of American politics—is refreshingly free of ideological involvements. It addresses palpable problems by whatever means lie to hand, relying on the power of *intellectual* technology to carry the day. And it looks to help whenever it can be found—and not necessarily only in the works of the "big names," at least as far as the domestic science is concerned.

The fact is that those bigger fish do not typify what the sea as a whole has to offer. Matters of philosophical history aside, some of the salient themes and issues with which American philosophers are grappling at the present time are

- applied ethics: ethical issues in the profession (medicine, business, law, etc.);
- computer issues: artificial intelligence, "can machines think?," the epistemology of information processing;
- rationality and its ramifications;

- social implications of medical technology (abortion, euthanasia, right to life, medical research issues, informed consent);

- feminist issues;

- social and economic justice, distributive policies, equality of opportunity, human rights;

- truth and meaning in mathematics and formalized languages;

- the merits and demerits of scepticism and relativism regarding knowledge and morality;

- the nature of personhood and the rights and obligations of persons.

None of these issues were put on the problem-agenda of present concern by any one particular philosopher. None arose out of a preoccupation with fundamental aspects of some already well established issue. None arose out of one particular philosophical text or discussion. They blossomed forth like the leaves of a tree in springtime appearing in various places at once under the formative impetus of the Zeitgeist of societal concern. The nature of American philosophy today is such that for the most part new ideas and tendencies have come to prominence not because of the influential impact of some specific contribution worker but because of the disaggregated effects of a host of writers working across a wide frontier of individual efforts. Philosophical innovation today is generally not the response to the preponderant effort of pace-setting individuals but a genuinely collective effort that is best characterized in statistical terms.

"But I really want to know what those bigger fish are thinking and teaching." Good for you! This interest of yours is perfectly appropriate—and laudable. But in pursuing it you must not fool yourself into thinking that the information you obtain is providing you with a satisfactory picture of American philosophy. For what you will be getting is no more than a pastiche of some philosophizing done by some Americans. To see this as somehow representative and possessed of some broader cultural significance—as usefully informative about the philosophical lay of the land in America at large—would be profoundly erroneous. Even a full account of the philosophical work of the two or three dozen of most influential American philosophers would not yield a faithful portrait of the present state of American philosophy at large, as reflected in the thematic structure of the present literature, the make-up of instructional curricula, or the constitution of conference programs.

Agenda-enlargement is yet another of the most striking features of contemporary American philosophy. The pages of its journals and the programs of its meetings bristle with discussions of issues that would seem bizarre to their predecessors of earlier days and to present-day philosophers of other places. For example, the overall program of the annual meeting of the Eastern Division of American Philosophical Association in December of 1991 included papers on "Is it Dangerous to Demystify Human Rights?," "Difference and the Differend in Derrida and Lyotard," "Animal Rights Theory and the Diminishment of Infants," "On the Ecological Consequences of Alphabetical Literacy," "Is Polygamy Good Feminism?," "The Ethics of the Free Market," "Planetary Projection of the Multiple Self on Films," "The Moral Collapse of the University," and "The Construction of Female Political Identity."[16] Entire societies are dedicated to the pursuit of issues now deemed philosophical that no one would have dreamt of considering so a generation ago. (Some examples are the societies for Machines and Mentality, for Informal Logic and Critical Thinking, for the Study of Ethics and Animals, for Philosophy and Literature, for Analytical Feminism, and for Philosophy of Sex and Love.) The fact that those many hundreds of philosophers are looking for something to do that is not simply a matter of reexploring familiar ground has created a substantial population pressure for more philosophical Lebensraum.

The result of this agenda-enlargement has been a revolutionizing of the structure of philosophy itself by way of taxonomic complexification. The current (1990s) picture of taxonomic lay of the land in North America philosophy is thus vastly more complex and ramified than anything that has preceded it. The tabulation of Appendix 5 gives an overview of the situation, which reflects the burgeoning of philosophical study and writing after World War II. The taxonomy of the subject has burst for good and all the bounds of the ancient tripartite scheme of logic, metaphysics and ethics. Specialization and division of labor runs rampant, and cottage industries are the order of the day. The situation has grown so complex and diversified that the most comprehensive recent English-language encyclopedia of philosophy[17] cautiously abstains from providing any taxonomy of philosophy whatsoever. (This phenomenon also goes a long way towards explaining why no one has written a comprehensive history of philosophy that carries through to the present-day scene.[18]) Philosophy—which ought by mission and tradition to be an integration of knowledge—has itself become increasingly disintegrated. The growth of the discipline has forced it beyond the limits of feasible surveillance by a single mind. After World War II it becomes literally impossible for American philosophers to keep up with what their colleagues were writing.

The rapid growth of "applied philosophy"—that is, philosophical reflection about detailed issues in science, law, business, social affairs, computer use, and the like—is a striking structural feature of contemporary North American philosophy. In particular, the past three decades have seen a great proliferation of narrowly focused philosophical investigations of particular issues in areas such as economic justice, social welfare, ecology, abortion, population policy, military defense, and so on. This situation illustrates the most characteristic feature of contemporary English-language philosophizing: the emphasis on detailed investigation of special issues and themes. For better or for worse, Anglophone philosophers have in recent years tended to stay away from large-scale abstract matters of wide and comprehensive scope, characteristic of the earlier era of Whitehead or Dewey, and nowadays incline to focus their investigations on issues of small-scale detail that relate to and grow out of those larger issues of traditional concern. The turning of philosophy from globally general, large-scale issues to more narrowly focused investigations of matters of microscopically fine-grained detail is a characteristic feature of American philosophy after World War II. Its flourishing use of the case-study method in philosophy is a striking phenomenon for which no one philosopher can claim credit—to a contemporary observer it seems like the pervasively spontaneous expression of "the spirit of the times."

In line with the increasing specialization and division of labor, American philosophy has become increasingly technical in character. Philosophy historians are increasingly preoccupied with matters of small-scale philosophical and conceptual microdetail. And philosophical investigations make increasingly extensive use of the formal machinery of semantics, modal logic, compilation theory, learning theory, etc. Ever heavier theoretical armaments are brought to bear on ever smaller problem-targets in ways that journal readers will occasionally wonder whether the important principle that technicalities should never be multiplied beyond necessity has been lost sight of. There is certainly no doubt that the increasing technicalization of philosophy has been achieved at the expense of its wider accessibility—and indeed even to its accessibility to members of the profession. No single thinker commands the whole range of knowledge and interests that characterizes present-day American philosophy, and indeed no single university department is so large as to have on its faculty specialists in every branch of the subject. The field has outgrown the capacity not only of its practitioners but even of its institutions.

Do American philosophers exert influence? Here, of course, the critical question is: Upon whom? First consider: upon *other philosophers*. We have already remarked that the extent to which even "the leading philosophers" manage to influence others is highly fragmentary—in each case only a small sector of the entire group being involved. Turning now to *the wider society at large*, it must be said that the answer is emphatically negative. American philosophers are not opinion-shapers: they do not have access to the media, to the political establishment, to the "think tanks" that seek to mold public opinion. Insofar as they exert an external influence at all, it is confined to *academics* of other fields. Professors of government may read John Rawls, professors of literature Richard Rorty, professors of linguistics W. V. Quine. But, outside the academy, the writings of such important contemporary American philosophers exert no influence. It was otherwise earlier in the century—in the era of philosophers like William James, John Dewey, and George Santayana—when the writings of individual philosophers set the stage for at least some discussions and debates among a wider public. But it is certainly not so in the America of today. Philosophers (and academics in general) play very little role in the molding of an "informed public opinion" in the U.S.—such work is largely done by publicists, filmmakers, and talk-show hosts. American society today does not reflect the concerns of philosophers but the very reverse is the case—where "relevant" at all, the writings of philosophers reflect the concerns of the society.

Many philosophers are not enthusiastic about this. For American philosophers by and large see themselves, accurately enough, as cultivating one academic specialty in contrast to others—as technicians working in the realm of ideas. And this means that they generally write for an audience of their fellow academics and have little interest in (or prospect of) addressing a wider public of intelligent readers at large. (This is another significant difference between the philosophical situation in North America and in continental Europe.) American philosophy is oriented to academia and academics. By contrast, European—and especially French—philosophy is oriented to the wider culture-complex of an intelligent readership through a concern with currently controverted issues. On this basis "political correctness," which has become a hotbed of controversy on various American campuses, has made comparatively little impact among philosophers—unlike the situation with practitioners of such fields as legal or literary theory. Outside of rather limited circles, philosophers in America are still expected to give reasons for their contentions, rather than painting those who dissent with the brush of fashionably attuned disapproval—let alone by calling names. The high degree of its technical professionalism has tended to countervail against the pervasive politicization of the field.

The prominence of specialization gives a more professional and technical cast to contemporary American philosophizing in comparison to that of other times and places. It endows the enterprise with something of that can-do spirit that one encounters in other aspects of American life. There is something of an optimistic confidence in the power of technique to resolve the problems of the field. In this respect American philosophizing has little use for a pessimism that contents itself with a melancholic resignation to human inadequacies. Confined to the precincts of higher education, contemporary American philosophy cannot easily afford sending messages that the young are not prepared to hear.

All the same, its increasing specialization has impelled philosophy towards the ivory tower. And so, the most recent years have accordingly seen something of a fall from grace of philosophy in American culture—not that there was ever all that much grace to fall from. For many years, the *Encyclopaedia Britannica* published an annual supplement entitled *19XY Book of the Year*, dealing with the events of the previous year under such rubrics as World Politics, Health, Music, etc. Until the 1977 volume's coverage of the preceding year's developments, a section of philosophy was always included in this annual series. But thereafter, philosophy vanished—without so much as a word of explanation. Seemingly the year of America's bicentennial saw the disappearance of philosophy from the domain of things that interest Americans. At approximately the same time, *Who's Who in America* drastically curtailed its coverage of philosophers (and academics generally). And during this same time period, various vehicles of public opinion—ranging from *Time* magazine to the *New York Times*—voiced laments over the irrelevance of contemporary philosophy to the problems of the human condition and the narcissistic absorption of philosophers in logical and linguistic technicalities that rendered the discipline irrelevant to the problems and interests of nonspecialists.[19] It is remarkable that this outburst of popular alienation from philosophy's ivory-towerishness came at just the time when philosophers in the U.S. were beginning to turn with relish to the problems on the agenda of public policy and personal concern. The flowering of applied ethics (medical ethics, business ethics, environmental ethics, and the like), of virtue ethics (trust, hope, neighborliness, etc.), of social ethics (distributive justice, privacy, individual rights, etc.) and of such philosophical hyphenations as philosophy-and-society—and even philosophy-and-agriculture!—can also be dated from just this period. By one of those ironies not uncommon in the pages of history, philosophy returned to the issues of the day at virtually the very moment when the wider public gave up thinking of the discipline as relevant to its concerns.

The fact is that philosophy has little or no place in American popular (as opposed to *academic*) culture, since at this level people's impetus to global understanding is accommodated—in America, at least—by religion rather than philosophy. Philosophical issues are by nature complicated, and Americans do not relish complications and have a marked preference for answers over questions. The nature of the case is such that philosophers must resort to careful distinctions and saving qualifications. And in this regard Americans do not want to know where the complexities lurk but yearn for the proverbial one-armed experts who do not constantly say "on the other hand." We are a practical people who want efficient solutions (as witness the vast market for self-help books with their dogmatic nostrums).

However, while philosophy nowadays makes virtually no impact on the wider culture of North America, its place in higher education is secure. To be sure, of all undergraduates in

American colleges and universities, only about half of one percent *major* in philosophy (compared with nearly three percent for English and over fifteen percent for business and management).[20] But owing to philosophy's role in meeting "distribution requirements" it has secured a prominent place in curriculum of post-secondary education. Unlike the United Kingdom, where post-World War II philosophers held a very technical and narrowly conceived idea of what the job of philosophy is—with the result of effectively assuring the discipline's declining role in the educational system—in America philosophy has managed not only to survive but to thrive in higher education. It has done so in large measure by taking a practicalist and accommodationist turn. American philosophers have been very flexible in bending with the wind. When society demands "relevancy to social concerns" a new specialty of "applied philosophers" springs forth to provide it. When problems of medical ethics or of feminist perspectivism occupy the society, a bevy of eager young philosophical spirits stands ready to leap into the breach.

And so, there is no question that philosophy is alive and well in America today. As long as it maintains its place in collegiate education with at least two or three competent representatives at each of those several thousand institutions that grant baccalaureate degrees, it will continue as an active and productive venture.

It should occasion no surprise that philosophical activity flourishes on the American academic scene in a way that reflects wider social concerns. Of the forty-five thematic sessions on the program of the American Philosophical Association's Eastern Division in 1991, six were devoted to feminist themes and two to issues relating to blacks.[21] This dedication of some fifteen percent of program space to these issues prominent on the agenda of present-day U.S. politics is clearly not accidental, but it does not reflect a comparable prominence of these topics in the current journal literature of the subject, where (as the *Philosopher's Index* entries indicate) the aggregate space occupied by these themes is diminutive. To a cynic, it might seem that American philosophers are seeking to offset the underrepresentation of women and blacks in their ranks by throwing words at the issues involved. (In this regard philosophers are akin to politicians, a consideration that invites second thoughts about Plato's philosopher-kings.)

Sometimes, however, what at first sight looks like a large-scale phenomenon is only the large shadow cast by a smallish object. This seems to be the case with feminist philosophy in North America. At present there are only two journals in the field (*Feminist Studies, Hypatia*) and only two societies (*Society for Analytical Feminism, Society for Women in Philosophy*). As far as philosophy goes, academic feminism, however prominent elsewhere, is at present still no more than a statistically minor blip.[22] (To be sure, the shift from nothing to something is always a big one.)

Insofar as American philosophers collect themselves into biological groupings of (comparatively) substantial size, this conformation is based not on factors of substance (of doctrinal agreement) but on factors of style (of methodological commonality). One major grouping—the "Analysts" as they have come to be called—adopts a scientific model of philosophizing and looks to the sort of detailed investigation by logico-linguistic methods of analysis that was introduced into Anglo-American philosophy in the era of G. E. Moore and Bertrand Russell. The other major affinity grouping—the "Pluralists"—look to continental models of philosophizing through reappraisals of the grand tradition of Western philosophy in the manner prominent in German philosophy in the era from Dilthey to Heidegger. Different culture-heroes are at issue, and different modes of procedure. The one "school" seeks to use the machinery of logic and formal semantics to extract philosophical juice from science and common sense, the other employs the methodology of historical and humanistic studies to extract lessons from the materials of cultural and intellectual history. The upshot is a difference in the substance of philosophizing that roots in a difference in the style of philosophical practice engendered by looking to rather different models of philosophizing. (However, the recent trend towards specialization and the division of labor is just as prominent among the pluralists as among the analysts.) Analysts often as not focus upon doctrines rather than writers. They generally discuss intellectual artifacts in the manner of the introduction, "I take a realist to be someone who endorses the following three theses..." where no actual person has ever propounded those theses together in exactly that form. By contrast, the "continental" style of philosophizing addresses the real (or supposedly real) views of identified philosophers—with different writers having somewhat different ideas about membership in the list of canonical authorities, each having a personal register of the good and the wicked.

An interesting—and unexpected—aspect of contemporary American philosophy relates to the fate of "pragmatism." The high priests of this quintessentially American tendency of thought—C. S. Peirce, William James, John Dewey, and C. I. Lewis—while entertaining rather different conceptions of the doctrine at issue, were all agreed on the central point that there is a cogent *standard* for assessing the merit for cognitive products (ideas, theories, methods)—a standard whose basis of validity reaches outside the realm of pure theory into the area of practical application and implementation. For them the ultimate test of our intellectual artifacts lay in seeing them of instrumentalities of effective praxis—in their ability to serve the communal purposes for whose sake and publicity available resources are instituted. But in recent years many philosophers who have laid claim to the label of "pragmatism" have subjected the traditional doctrine to a drastic sea change. Where the classical pragmatists sought in applicative efficacy a test of objective adequacy—an individual-transcending reality principle to offset the vagaries of personal reactions—the pseudo-pragmatists turn their backs on the pursuit of objectivity and impersonality. For traditional pragmatism's communal concern with "what works out *for us* (humans in general)" they have perversely substituted an egocentrism of "what works out *for me* (or *for you*)." The defining object of the pragmatic tradition—the search for objective and impersonal standards—is shattered into a fragmentation of individual impressions in the parochial setting of a limited culture context. We have a total dissolution—that is, destruction—of the classical pragmatic approach that saw the rational validity of intellectual artifacts to reside in the capacity to provide effective guidance in the successful conduct of our extra-theoretical affairs—in matters of prediction, planning, successful intervention in the course of nature, and other such-like aspects of the successful conduct of our practical activities.

The large ongoing response to writers such as Heidegger, Derrida, and their epigones clearly shows that there is more academic hay to be made nowadays by debunking metaphysics and epistemology as traditionally conceived than by practicing them. In this light, one of the striking and paradoxical features of American philosophy today is the widespread assault by a disaffected avant-garde against the discipline as standardly practiced. On many fronts a *fin de siècle* disillusionment with the enterprise is coming to expression and a distaste for actual scholarship is widely manifest among the avant-garde. Some argue—be it on the basis of scepticism or relativism or scientism—that we have entered a "post-philosophical era," where philosophy as traditionally conceived is no longer viable. Others argue on neo-Marxist grounds that interest (not necessarily economic but also cultural or social) is what determines all and that old-style would-be rational philosophy is simply a covering for sexist, racist, or culturalist prejudices. Traditional philosophizing is viewed as mere ideology that should be dismissed as the prejudicial vaporings of dead white males, and the politically correct thing to do is to abandon philosophy as a venture in inappropriate elitism.[23] Other critiques of philosophizing issue from a philosophy-external basis. Followers of the "critical studies" trend of literacy analysis propose to deconstruct philosophical discourse to a point of a variety that renders rational deliberation unrealizable.[24] From the vantage point of such a "postmodernist" disdain for reason, traditional philosophy's commitment to the methodology of reflective analysis and impartial reasonableness continues to earn for it the sort of opposition encountered by Socrates at the very outset of the enterprise. However, the fact that any critical examination of the scope and merits of philosophy will itself form part of the philosophical venture at large—that metaphilosophy is a part of philosophy—continues to assure the discipline with a lively future despite all such critical opposition.[25]

Insofar as this descriptive survey admits of an overall interpretation, it is somewhat as follows. A century ago, the historian Henry Adams deplored the end of the predominance of the great and the good in American politics and the emergence of a new order based on the dominance of masses and their often self-appointed representatives. Control of the political affairs of the nation was flowing from the hands of a cultural elite into that of the unimposing, albeit vociferous, spokesmen for the faceless masses. In short, democracy was setting in. Exactly this same transformation from the preeminence of great figures to the predominance of mass movements is now, one hundred years on, the established situation in even so intellectual an enterprise as philosophy. In its present configuration, American philosophy indicates that the "revolt of the masses," which Ortega y Gasset thought characteristic of our era, manifests itself not only in politics and social affairs but in intellectual culture also and even in philosophy.[26] A cynic might characterize the current situation as a victory of the troglodytes over the giants.[27] The condition of American philosophy today is a matter of trends and fashions that go their own way without the guidance of agenda-controlling individuals. This results in a state of affairs that calls for description on a statistical rather than biographical basis. It is ironic to see the partisans of political correctness in academia condemning philosophy as an elitist discipline at the very moment when philosophy itself has abandoned elitism and succeeded in making itself over in a populist reconstruction. American philosophy has now well and truly left "the genteel tradition" behind.

If such a perspective is indeed valid, certain far-reaching implications follow for the eventual historiography of present-day American philosophy. For it indicates a situation with which no historian of philosophy has as yet come to terms. In the "heroic" era of the past, the historian of the philosophy of a place and time could safely concentrate upon the *dominant* figures and expect thereby to achieve a certain completeness with respect to "what really mattered." But such an approach is grossly unsuited to the conditions of the present era. Those "dominant figures" have lost control of the agenda. To accommodate the prevailing realities, the story of present-day American philosophy must be presented in a much more aggregated and statistically articulated format. And insofar as single individuals are dealt with as such, it must be done against such an enlarged background—they must now be seen as *representative* rather than as *determinative* figures, with the status of the individual philosopher selected for historical consideration generally downgraded into a merely exemplary (illustrative) instance of a larger trend. The historian of American philosophy in its present-day configuration accordingly faces a task of selection entirely different in nature and scope from that which prevailed heretofore. If the development of American philosophy continues along its present path, the role of the individual in the historiography of the future will be as the subject of a footnote illustrative of the diversified general trends and tendencies of thought to which the main body of the text will have to be dedicated.

American philosophy, then, is very much alive. But is it also well and healthy? Should one welcome or deplore the confused and dissonant scene we find about us? Should the circumstance that present-day American philosophers almost invariably write for other philosophers rather than addressing a wider public of intelligent lay readers not be seen as a substantial a demerit of the enterprise?

The fact is that there is little point in lamenting what cannot be helped: one must accept the inevitable. And in the present case the structure of the situation allows no alternatives. Ten able thinkers of varying background, experience, instruction, and prejudices are surely not going to reach consensus on major ideological issues—let alone ten thousand of them. Nor, in a society that prioritizes the pursuit of happiness and divides its ideological inclinations between life's practicalities on the one hand and pie-in-the-sky idealism on the other, will philosophy's half-way house ever be genuinely popular. American philosophers must take their readership where they find it, and this will not be among the wider public but rather among their colleagues—and also, of course, among that captive audience, their students. Accordingly, American philosophy today is characterized not by uniformity and cohesion but by a luxuriant diversity that offers something to suit most every taste. This pluralistic character of American philosophy represents a realistic and effective accommodation to its environing circumstances and conditions. And that, after all, is what health is all about.[28, 29]

Appendix 1

MEMBERSHIP IN THE AMERICAN
PHILOSOPHICAL ASSOCIATION

1965	2,624
1970	2,725
1975	2,888
1980	5,194
1985	6,874
1990	8,792

SOURCE: Personal communication from the American Philosophical
Association Secretariat.

NOTE 1: A disproportionately large part of this membership expansion
has occurred in the Pacific (i.e., far-western) Division.

NOTE 2: This increase of 235% in APA membership contrasts with an
increase of 130% in undergraduate enrollments and an
increase of 30% in the general population. (Data from
Statistical Abstracts of the United States, 1992 [Washington,
D.C.: Bureau of the Census, 1992], pp. 163-65.) Like
Americans in general, American philosophers have proven
themselves to be markedly entrepreneurial.

Appendix 2

PHILOSOPHY'S PART IN U.S. DOCTORATES

	All Doctorates	Doctorates in Letters Fields +	Total	Philosophy Doctorates Men	Philosophy Doctorates Women	Philosophy as % of Ph.D.s	Philosophy as % of Letters Ph.D.s
1970-71	32,107	2,416	394	358	36	2.0%	16.3%
1972-73	34,777	2,754	409	344	65	1.2%	14.9%
1974-75	34,083	2,495	375	318	57	1.1%	15.0%
1976-77	33,232	2,191	330	264	66	1.0%	15.0%
1978-79	32,730	1,919	258	204	54	0.8%	13.4%
1980-81	32,958	1,790	280	224	56	0.8%	15.6%
1982-83	32,775	1,580	232	170	62	0.7%	14.7%
1984-85	32,943	1,707	234	191	43	0.7%	13.7%
1986-87	34,839	1,180	222	172	50	0.6%	18.8%

+Including Philosophy and Religion. Contrast categories: Life Sciences,
Physical Sciences, Social Sciences.

Appendix 3

MAJOR Ph.D. PRODUCING DEPARTMENTS
IN THE UNITED STATES AND CANADA: 1986-1991

(Departments whose Ph.D. programs awarded at least 24 philosophy
doctorates in the five academic years from 1986-87 to 1990-91)

Most Productive Institutions	Number of Philosophy Doctorates (1986-1991)
Boston College	24
Brown University	29
Columbia University	28
Georgetown University	28
Guelph/McMaster University Joint Program	24
Notre Dame University	25
SUNY at Stony Brook	29
University of Massachusetts	28
University of Minnesota	24
University of Pittsburgh	26
University of Texas	30
University of Toronto	36
University of Wisconsin	32
Vanderbilt University	28

IVY LEAGUE COMPARISON

Columbia University	28
Harvard	20
Princeton	21
University of Pennsylvania	18
Yale	19

NOTE: The "Catholic Big Five" (Boston College, Catholic University of
America, Fordham, Georgetown, Notre Dame) outproduced the
five "Ivy League" universities by 114 to 106 during this period.

SOURCE: Data from the annual survey in the September issue of
The Review of Metaphysics.

Appendix 4

OFT-CITED AMERICAN PHILOSOPHERS

This listing includes those living American philosohers
who have 100 or more combined entries for 1990 and 1991
in the *Humanities Citation Index*.

Adams, Robert M.	116	Kuhn, Thomas	520
Alston, William P.	103	Laudan, Larry	177
Bennett, Jonathan	126	Lewis, David	429
Cavell, Stanley	201	MacIntyre, Alasdair	405
Chisholm, Roderick	177	Nagel, Thomas	255
Danto, Arthur	193	Nozick, Robert	192
Davidson, Donald	456	Nussbaum, Martha	168
Dennett, Daniel	191	Plantinga, Alvin	132
Dreyfus, Hubert	148	Putnam, Hilary	461
Elster, Jon	201	Quine, W. V.	502
Feyerabend, Paul	196	Rawls, John	474
Goodman, Nelson	315	Rescher, Nicholas	129
Hacking, Ian	155	Rorty, Richard	684
Harman, Gilbert	137	Searle, John	204
Hartshorne, Charles	138	Smith, John	139
Hempel, Carl G.	155	Taylor, Charles	228
Hintikka, Jaakko	136	Toulmin, Stephen	142
Kripke, Saul	237	Williams, Bernard	308

SOME EUROPEAN COMPARISONS

Derrida, Jacques	1,982	Hare, Richard M.	191
Dummett, Michael	178	Popper, Karl R.	507
Gadamer, Jans-Georg	521	Ricoeur, Paul	703
Habermas, Jürgen	1,124	Strawson, Peter F.	145

NOTE 1: It has to be remembered that these citation statistics represent not just the quality of contributions but the fashions of the community. Moreover, the difference between the Anglo-American and the Continentals to some extent reflects the greater relevance of the writings of the latter to the work of their fellow humanists at large.

NOTE 2: It is worth noting that almost a quarter of the Americans are immigrants to North America. This indicates, among other things, both the openness of American universities and their dependence on imported talent.

Appendix 5

THE SUBDIVISIONS OF PHILOSOPHY (ca. 1990)

Object of Consideration	Branch of Philosophy
God	Philosophy of Religion/ Philosophical Theology
Nature ("the physical world" and "the biological world")	Metaphysics/Philosophy of Nature
Mankind	
—"the human condition" in general	Philosophical Anthropology
—the human mind and its operation	Philosophy of Mind/ Philosophical Psychology
Society (community)	Social Philosophy/ Political Philosophy
—social policy	Philosophy of Public Policy
—cultural perspectives	Feminist Philosophy Black Studies re. Philosophy
Individuals	
—re. action and interaction in their ethical dimension	
At large	Ethics (personal)/ Moral Philosophy
In special contexts	Applied Ethics
	• Medical Ethics
	• Business Ethics
	• Bioethics
	• (others)
re. thought	(see the rubric *Artifacts* below)
Artifacts: Processes (Mechanisms/Methods/Methodology)	
—Cognitive	Theory of Knowledge/ Epistemology/Methodology of Inquiry
	Theory of Everyday Knowledge/ General Epistemology
	Theory of Experience (Phenomenology)
	Theory of Evaluation (Value Theory, Axiology)
	Theory of Demonstrative Inference (Deductive Logic)

Appendix 5 (cont.)

Object of Consideration	Branch of Philosophy
	Theory of Inductive Inference (Inductive Logic)
	Theory of Scientific Method
	Theory of Rational Discourse (Dialectics)
	Theory of Probabilistic and Plausible Reasoning
	Theory of Interpretation (Hermeneutics)
	Theory of Learning (Philosophy of Education)
	(others)
−Behavioral	
Linguistic	Philosophy of Language
	Philosophy of Communication Processes
Non-Linguistic	Theory of Action (Praxiology, Action Theory, Decision Theory, Theory of Rational Choice and Preference, etc.)
	Philosophy of Sport
Artifacts: Products	Philosophy of Natural Science (with subdivisions by special sciences)
	Philosophy of Social Sciences
	• Philosophy of Economics
	• Philosophy of History/Historiography
	• Philosophy of Law (Jurisprudence)
	Philosophy of the Formal Sciences
	• Philosophy of Logic
	• Philosophy of Mathematics
	Philosophy of Culture and Humanistic Learning (of the "Arts")
	• Philosophy of Art (Aesthetics)
	• Philosophy of Literature
	• Philosophy of Philosophy (Metaphilosophy)
	Philosophy of Physical Production (of the "Crafts")
	• Philosophy of Work
	• Philosophy of Technology

Notes

1. This essay is an expanded revision of a lecture on "The State of North American Philosophy Today" delivered at the Pontifical University of Salamanca in April of 1992. This presentation was followed by a lively discussion that stretched my knowledge of Spanish to—nay even beyond—its limits. I want to emphasize here that I do not necessarily welcome the various facts which this essay tries to describe more or less objectively. However, I found it an instructive exercise to try to see American philosophy from the vantage point of an external perspective.

2. Bruce Kuklik, *The Rise of American Philosophy: 1860-1930* (New Haven: Yale University Press, 1977).

3. For reasons less of cultural imperialism than of substantive similitude and scholarly kinship, U.S. and Canadian philosophizing has been aggregated into one overarching "North American" whole for the purposes of the present discussion. Perhaps this overlooks some subtle differences in approach—even as U.S. and Canadian spoken English exhibit subtle differences. But from a Hispanic—let alone an Iberian—vantage point these differences are insignificant.

4. Of the three top "Ivy League" institutions (Yale, Harvard, and Princeton), none presently has more than one woman full professor in its philosophy department. And this state of affairs is in general rather the rule than the exception.

5. See D. D. Karnos and R. G. Schoemaker (eds.), *Falling in Love With Wisdom: [62] American Philosophers Talk about Their Calling* (New York & Oxford: Oxford University Press, 1993). From this interesting anthology one must conclude that while American philosophers are driven, surprisingly many are not driven by that curiosity and wonder which, as Aristotle has it, lies at the core of philosophizing.

6. There is a considerable diversity of explanations of the nature of philosophizing that would account for the diversified qualifications of projects and positions that actually exists. Cf. the author's *The Strife of Systems* (Pittsburgh: University of Pittsburgh Press, 1985).

7. See the essay by Bruce Kuklick, "Does American Philosophy Rest on a Mistake?" in Marcus G. Singer (ed.), *American Philosophy* (Cambridge: Cambridge University Press, 1985; Royal Institute of Philosophy Lecture Series, No. 19), pp. 177-89.

8. The scattershot nature of recent American philosophy is illustrated—among innumerable examples—by the 1970 volume entitled *The Future of Metaphysics*, edited by Robert E. Wood (Chicago: Quadrangle Books). Not only are the seventeen contributors disagreed as to the future of metaphysics, they are in dissensus about its past as well: what the definitive tasks of the field are, which practitioners afford the best role models, and which approaches have proved to be the most promising.

9. See the *Directory of American Philosophers*, 1992-93 (Bowling Green: Philosophy Documentation Center), pp. 176-91.

10. For one (perfectly average) month, October of 1991, the "Philo-

sophical Calendar" of the American Philosophical Association listed the following events: (1) Conference on System and Teleology in Kant's *Critique of Judgment* at Memphis State University; (2) Mountain-Plains Philosophy Conference at Colorado State University; (3) American Maritain Association colloquium, in Washington, D.C.; (4) Society for Health and Human Values meeting in St. Louis, Missouri; (5) Virginia Philosophical Association meeting in Norfolk, Virginia; (6) Society for Phenemology and Existential Philosophy meeting in Memphis, Tennessee; (7) Conference on Social Theory, Politics and the Arts in Jacksonville, Florida; (8) International John MacMurry Society meeting at Marquette University, Milwaukee, Wisconsin; (9) Midwest Radical Scholars Conference, Loyola University, Chicago, Illinois; (10) Wheaton College Philosophy Conference, Wheaton, Illinois; (11) Tenth Annual Joint Meeting of the Society for American Greek Philosophy and the Society for the Study of Islamic Philosophy and Science, Baruch College, New York, New York.

11. Data from Fritz Machlup, *et al.*, *Information Through the Printed Word*, vol. I (New York: Praeger, 1978), p. 238.

12. *Directory of American Philosophers, op. cit.*, pp. 192-216.

13. Edward B. Fiske, "Lessons," *The New York Times* (August 2, 1989), p. B8. At this rate, the annual output of Shakespearian scholarships is over six times as large as the collected works of the Bard himself.

14. Salary data for 1990-91 from *Academe*, vol. 77 (1991), pp. 9-17.

15. The process at issue relates to the principle known in the social sciences as Rousseau's Law, maintaining that in a population of size n the number of high-visibility members stands as the square root of n. Compare the author's *Scientific Progress* (Oxford: Blackwell, 1978), pp. 96ff. On its telling, in a profession of 10,000 we would expect to find some hundred widely recognized contributors.

16. *Proceedings and Addresses of the American Philosophical Association*, vol. 65, no. 2 (October 1991), pp. 13-41.

17. *The Encyclopedia of Philosophy*, edited by Paul Edwards (London & New York: Macmillan, 1967).

18. John Passmore's *Recent Philosophers* (La Salle: Open Court, 1985) is as close as anything we have, but—as the very title indicates—this excellent survey makes no pretentions to comprehensiveness. In this direction an earlier multi-person survey went somewhat further, exemplifying what is the best and most that one can hope to obtain: Roderick M. Chisholm *et al.*, *Philosophy: Princeton Studies of Humanistic Scholarship in America* (Englewood Cliffs, NJ: Prentice-Hall, 1964). Yet not only does this book attest to the fragmentation of the field—but it conveys (from its Foreword onwards) the defeatist suggestion that whatever larger lessons can be extracted from an historically minded scrutiny of the substantive diversity of the contemporary situation are destined to lie substantially in the eyes of the beholder.

19. See *TIME* magazine, Essay: "What (If Anything) to Expect from Today's Philosophers," vol. 87 (January 7, 1966), pp. 24-25.

20. Data from Carnegie Foundation for the Advancement of Teaching,

entitled *Carnegie Survey of Undergraduates, 1986*, as reported in *The Chronicle of Higher Education*, February 5, 1986, pp. 27-30.

21. *Proceedings and Addresses of the American Philosophical Association*, vol. 65, no. 2 (October 1991), pp. 11ff.

22. Cf. Appendixes 4 and 5.

23. Cornel West, for one, regards the reluctance of American philosophers to abandon classical issues and methods as betokening the fuddy-duddy adherence of "an American male WASP cultural elite loyal to an older and eroding European model of culture" and as a resistance to taking the plunge into the invigorating atmosphere of a "prophetic...form of American left thought and action in our post-modernist moment" (*The American Evasion of Philosophy* [Madison: University of Wisconsin Press, 1989]; see pp. 238-39).

24. To be sure, that does not trouble them, since they see rationality itself as a form of political oppression, given the hyperdemocratic consideration that while everyone *feels* only some of us trouble to *think*.

25. The enthusiasm with which philosophers co-opt the issue of the infeasibility of philosophizing is illustrated in the recent anthology edited by Avener Cohen and Marcelo Descal under the title *The Institution of Philosophy: A Discipline in Crisis* (La Salle: Open Court, 1989).

26. Where Ortega himself did not expect it: "Philosophy needs no protection, no attention, no sympathy, no interest in the part of the masses. Its perfect uselessness protects it" (*The Revolt of the Masses*, translated by Anthony Kerrigan [Notre Dame: University of Notre Dame Press, 1989], p. 73). Ortega did not reckon with "applied philosophy."

27. The General Editor of a first-rate survey of American humanistic scholarship wrote in the Foreword to the volume on philosophy: "Not many of the names mentioned in these pages are recognizable as those of great intellectual leaders, and many are unknown even to an old academic hand like myself who has a fair speaking acquaintance with the various humanistic disciplines in America" (Richard Schlatter in Roderick Chisholm *et al.*, *Philosophy: Princeton Studies of Humanistic Scholarship in America* [*op. cit.*], p. x).

28. I am grateful to Jon Mandle and Annamarie Marrow for their help in gathering information for the appendixes. And I am indebted to Richard Gale, John Kekes, and Laura Ruetsche for constructively critical comments.

29. This chapter is a slightly revised version of an essay initially published in *The Review of Metaphysics*, vol. 46 (1993), pp. 717-45.

Chapter Two

THE RISE AND FALL OF
ANALYTIC PHILOSOPHY

1. The Inspirations of
Anglo-American Analytic Philosophy

ANGLO-AMERICAN analytic philosophy is not so much a philosophical position as an approach to the issues, an ideology as to how work in the field is properly to be done. At its basis lies a view of the proper way to conduct philosophical inquiry and a pre-vision of the results of this way of proceeding.

Perhaps the best way to understand the nature of analytic philosophy as a doctrinal stance is through a consideration of the particular theses and theories that provided its initial impetus. A series of particular studies were especially influential in existing a formative influence with respect to the analytical approach. The highlights of this process are the following.

Russell on nonexistents. In his classic 1905 paper "On the Logic of Denotation," Bertrand Russell maintained that it is a fundamental mistake to project an ontology of nonexistent objects—as Meinong, for example, endeavored to do. Russell insisted that *the present king of France* is not a nonexistent object of some sort, but rather that all there is is the *expression* "the present king of France" which functions in a certain particular way in sentential contexts—a way that led to the consequences that *all* predicational statements of the type "The present king of France is bald" are false. The idea that we are here dealing with an *object* of some rather peculiar sort is a linguistic (rather that *optical*) illusion.

G. E. Moore on goodness. Moore's deliberations about the "meaning" of goodness led to the conclusion is that "the good" is an idea that must be understood in its own terms—that the meaning of this expression cannot be captured by a redefinitional formula of the format "The good is that which...(is happiness promoting, conducive to the greatest good of the greatest number, or the like) for a definitional clarification of 'the good' is predestined to futility." The philosophical quest (going back to Socrates) for a definitional speculation on the nature of goodness is a delusion. To be sure, this check is not a complete defeat for the clarificatory project. For we must distinguish between *definitions* and *explanations* of the good—and this between good-constituting and good-making characteristics. The former as a soluble problem: friendship, enjoyment, etc. By failing to be sufficiently mindful of the linguistic properties, philosophers have fruitlessly addressed the wrong issue. Moore saw this upshot as an intrinsic of a "paradox of analysis" inherent in the dilemma that a proposed analysis simply either *restates* (in which case it is otiose) or *misstates* (in which case it is incorrect). The attempts of philosophers to provide definitional clarifications thus often (perhaps always) issue in mistakes that a closer heed of the appropriate use of language can and should avert.

Einstein on space-time. The decidedly philosophical aspect of Einsteinian special relativity also brought grist to the analytic philosophers' mill. Given that no signal (and no natural process) could travel any faster than the velocity of light, there can be no way of implementing the idea of absolute simultaneity. And without simultaneously, Einstein's classic thought experiment of measurement by "traveling along a light ray" means that we are driven to a reliance on physical transmission processes (such as the motion of a light ray) in determining epistemological relations. This led to the conclusion that space-time not a physical container with a shape and structure of its own but simply a structural feature of natural occurrences. And this in turn substantiated the view that traditional science and philosophy have misunderstood the nature of something so basic as space and time and that an appropriate conceptual/scientific analysis can rectify so fundamental a (mis)conception.

Wittgenstein (early) on logical form. The prime object of Wittgenstein's *Tractatus* was to clarify the nature of factual claims about matters of existence. The *Tractatus* has it that factual propositions basically have a format (a "logical form") that can be *exhibited* (exemplified, instantiated) but not *explained* (definitionally encapsulated in some descriptive formula). As Wittgenstein sees it, philosophers have mistakenly thought they could explain the logical features of claims about the world's ultimate constraints. But these are matters where we can only show and not tell, and "whereof one cannot speak one must be silent."

F. P. Ramsey on truth. Philosophers have thought that they could explain the nature of truth. But a rational analysis of the matter shows that no definitional characterization is possible. All that we can manage is to only show how truth works—via a "redundancy account" that roots in the equivalence: "p" is true iff p. To pursue the idea of an explicative analysis of "the meaning of truth" (as a matter of accord with fact, or of coherence, or of assertoric, utility, or some such) is to chase an illusion. To claim the truth of an assertion is neither more nor less than to offer that assertion itself. A logically informed scrutiny of the issue shows that a definitional meaning restatement is infeasible. Traditional philosophical theories of truth (correspondence, coherence, etc.) have barked up the wrong tree. At this point, no profitable philosophical theorizing is possible.

Wittgenstein (late) on "meaning." Philosophers have sought to provide definitional formulas for the fundamental concepts of philosophical concern. But as Wittgenstein saw it, this project is doomed to futility. The phenomena at issue in this conceptual sphere are simply too complex and variegated to admit of capture in a most definitional net. Consider the conception of a "game." With games there simply is no uniform (essentialistic) commonality. All we have is a set of *family resemblances* among various sorts of games. No definitional characterization is possible; no philosophical theorizing is profitable. We have to disenchant philosophers from the captivity of procrustean theories of meaning. It is a mistake to see "knowledge" as a particular sort of commodity ("the *facts* that we appropriately recognize as such"). Rather, to know something is *to treat it* in a certain sort of way (*viz.,* to use it in one's own thinking and to stand prepared to convince others of it.)

Austin on knowledge. To seek to discern and specify the "nature of knowledge" is a mistake. The idea of knowledge is not an ideational resource with a conceptual core identity of some sort. Once again, knowledge is not so much a theoretical claim as a practical commitment. To claim that "I know p" is to make a commitment to issue a promissory note "you can rely on me, take my word for it, count on my being able to make good." (Hence "I know but may possibly be wrong" is simply absurd.) Philosophy elucidates nothing and explains nothing—it simply describes the realities of prevailing language use.

These teachings—and many others of the same general sort—provided the philosophical models towards which the philosophers of the analytic tradition looked in forming their view of the proper way in which work in this field should be conducted.[1]

2. The Doctrinal Views of Analytic Philosophy

The analytic manner of conducting philosophical inquiry exemplified in the various studies surveyed in the preceding section was accordingly taken by adherents to the analytical movement as conveying and substantiating a series of doctrinal lessons regarding the concept of understanding of the nature of philosophy:

1. *The enchantments of language.* Philosophical theses and theories in general reflect misconceptions and misunderstandings that arise out of linguistic misunderstandings. In fact, entire philosophical theories (doctrines) are often and perhaps even generally predicated on an insufficient appreciation of the linguistic proprieties and sophistications. Even where there is a single word (knowledge, truth, or whatever) there simply is not, in general, any such item at issue that one can appropriately wax philosophical about.

2. *Linguistic analysis as a philosophical anodyne.* The distress of philosophical perplexity and puzzlement can be removed by logico-linguistic analysis. A heed of the logical and linguistic realities will solve or dissolve our philosophical problems.

3. *Reduction to scientific residues.* After logico-linguistic misunderstandings have been removed from a domain of a philosophical concern, and philosophical misconceptions cleared away, whatever residual problems remain are scientific (formally or factually substantive) in nature. Thus even where appropriate analysis does not *dissolve* a philosophical problem, such analysis will reduce it to a residue that can and should be *resolved* by scientific means.

4. *The prioritizing of science.* In the final analysis, the only knowledge we (can) have that is significant (in both of this term's senses of *meaningful* and *worth knowing*) is scientific knowledge—either formal (logic, language-theoretic, mathematical) or factual (i.e., geared to the several natural and social sciences).

5. *The end of philosophical theorizing.* Accordingly, no characteristic substantive mission remains for philosophy as such. Traditional philosophical theorizing comes to an end as a distinct cognitive enterprise. It is a mistake to conceive of philosophy as a discipline—a sector of cognitive inquiry and theorizing. The turn to analysis brings philosophy as heretofore generally understood and practiced to a dead end. Traditional

philosophy is based on misunderstanding; its problems will either be dissolved through appropriate analysis or else transformed into issues that appropriately belong to the formal or factual sciences. All those time-worn philosophical disputes can be laid to rest in the light of analytical clarification of the relevant issues.

* * * *

Thus as the ideologues of the analytical school saw the matter, the only proper procedure in philosophizing is one of analysis issuing in the elimination (by way of dissolution or solution) of traditional philosophical problems as such. The analytical task is to deploy the instruments of logico-linguistic clarification to unmask philosophical issues either as the misunderstandings or as conceptual (rather than optical) illusions regarding what are actually scientific issues. Language analysis leads to the solution of philosophical problems by way of their elimination as such. The analysts accordingly saw themselves as iconoclasts using a new methodology—that of logic-linguistic analysis—to transform our understanding of philosophical issues in such a way as either to unravel them into the nothingness of linguistic misunderstanding or to transmute them into factual/scientific issues masquerading in a different and problematic disguise. Analytical philosophy accordingly looked to the dawning of a new day in the domain.

As is so often the case with philosophical doctrines, its prospect and teaching is most usefully clarified by considering the views and doctrines that it opposes. In this light, it is instructive to note that the analytical movement saw its principal opponents as follows:

1. *System builders*. Those philosophers who defended large-scale theories and systems, who were concerned for the production of big pictures rather than letting the larger scene simply emerge from a plethora of minutely detailed studies—those who demanded large-scale (global) rather than small scale (local) explanations.

2. *Philosophical autonomists*. Those who see philosophy as a substantive cognitive enterprise distinct from, and perhaps even co-equal with, the (formal and substantive) sciences—who take philosophical issues to be sufficiently independent of scientific ones as to endow the enterprise with the capacity to provide important information supplementary to the teachings

of science. Those who see philosophy as a substantively informative rather than a conceptually clarificatory enterprise.

3. *Respecters of history*. Those who think that the work of the great philosophers of days past conveys important insights into the truth of things; who do not see the present as discontinuous with the past in affording a new turning that makes all philosophizing that antedates the discovery of "the true method" obsolete and useless (apart from some occasional anticipations of contemporary insights).

4. *Sentimentalists*. Those traditional humanists who concede cognitive utility and probative authority to sentiment, feeling, tradition—indeed to anything outside the realm of the specifically conceptual and evidential sphere. Those who give a place of pride and prominence to the affective side of human experience and relegate objective impersonal observation to a subordinate place on the priority scale of philosophical significance and importance.

5. *Edificationists*. Those who think that a major task of philosophy is to deal with issues of *wisdom* (i.e., with the question of "How to live?") as something no less significant than the issues of knowledge (i.e., with the question of "What to think?").

What the analysts hoped to accomplish was to *épater les professeurs*, to discomfit the woolly-headed old-line philosophy professors who regarded themselves as guardians of a distinctive humanistic tradition. In deploying the tools of the formal sciences (logical and linguistic), the analysts saw themselves as delivering into the hands of hard-headed scientists a secure and permanent victory in their perennial struggles with the humanists (the practitioners of the mere *Geisteswissenschaften*). Analytic philosophy thus inclined towards a positivistic bias that regarded knowledge as the sole legitimate guardian of intellectual culture. As the movement's major adherents saw it, the task of the present is to bring in a post-philosophical era that does away with philosophizing as traditionally conceived and at last puts philosophy onto "the secure high-road of a science."

3. SHOCKS TO THE ANALYTICAL VISION

The basic building blocks of the program of the analytical "movement" were put in place by the philosophers of the first third of the century (Russell, Moore, Wittgenstein, Ramsey). Its working out of its development into a full-fledged program was the task of their successors in the second third of the century. It is easy to name *some* of the major contributors here (Ryle, Austin, Urmson, and Strawson in Britain and in the United States, Quine, C. I. Lewis, Frankena, Chisholm). But this is only the top of the tip of the iceberg. The movement became too popular and diffuse to admit of any compact register of its developers, who in fact were legion—and it also became intermingled with the logical positivists and the epistemologists of science.[2]

But as the program evolved, certain insights came to light with increasing clarity that gave rude shocks to main doctrinal views which had provided analytic philosophy's originative impetus.

1. *The fuzziness of the fundamental ideas at issue in analytic philosophy itself.* The infeasibility—largely elucidated in the work of Popper, Hempel, Quine, and Davidson—of achieving any clear distinctions in such analytically fundamentally contrasts as science/nonscience, analytic/synthetic, formal/factual, meaningful/meaningless. Indeed even such fundamental concepts as "philosophy," "language," "meaning," and their congeners resist all attempts at explanatory specification of what is at issue and dissolve into "loose clusters," "family resemblance groups," "essentially contented conceptions," or the like. The very terms of reference by whose means the philosophical analysts proposed to carry on their work seemed to dissolve into thin air as to elude their grasp. Take, for example—

2. *The complexity of knowledge.* Even if we cannot provide a redefinitional specification of the nature of knowledge we would certainly hope and expect to achieve some analytical clarification of the use conditions for assertions of the form "*X* knows that *P*." One promising suggestion that is as old as the suggestion in Plato's *Theaetetus* of the formula:

> "*X* knows that *P*" iff *P* is true and *X* believes that *P* and *X* has good grounds for believing that *P*.

But as the extensive discussion of the Russell-Gettier counterexamples to this formulation have shown, all of the promising attempts to provide such a use-condition specification soon came to grief. More and more epicycles of complexity had to be introduced into the analysis which even then never proved satisfactory.

3. *The fragmentation of logic.* The proliferation of logical systems was another stumbling block. The diversification of logico-linguistic instruments and the diversity of their modus operandi created so radically diversified a range of options that one can no longer appropriately speak in the singular of the proper analysis of a certain concept or statement or linguistic

usage. The complexity that Wittgenstein envisioned with respect to philosophical *concepts* holds also for philosophical *analyses*. And diverse instruments yield diverse products. Analysis does not provide the guideposts of a fixed conceptual pathway. There are virtually as many modes of analyses as there are analysts. How—after all—can we hope to achieve a uniquely "correct" logico-linguistic analysis when there are so many different such logico-linguistic systems?

4. *The recalcitrance of value.* It soon became apparent that no amount of clarification (analysis) of value language can reduce issues of right/wrong, just/unjust, important/unimportant to matters that are simply factual/scientific issues without any residue of issues that are themselves clearly evaluative. The endeavors to analyze value concepts—be they successful or otherwise—just do not address the substantive issues that are at stake in this domain.[3] Specifically, we confront—

5. *The bankruptcy of meta-ethics.* Philosophical analysis itself stresses and clarifies the gap between what is and what ought to be (between facts and values). But any meta-ethical analysis of how our ethical talk (or right/wrong, good/bad, honest/dishonest) describe facts of usage. And this affords us no gap in substantive ethical issues. But in the end, what actually interests us here is what *is* right and not what people *say* is right. Analytical meta-ethics' exclusive focus on the explication of usage leaves us with the grim choice between sidelining our ethical concerns.

The historical course of developments within the evaluation of analytic philosophy itself accordingly produced a series of bitter lessons for the program's adherents:

(1) *Analytic clarity produces complexification.* When we analyze the issues, the situation is not simplified/resolved. The issues when seen in greater detail are thereby seen to be more complex and variegated than was expected. Analysis does not dissolve or resolve the issues but makes them more complex and sophisticated. It does not lead to resolutement to fragmentation and proliferation. We thus face a—

(2) *Conservation of problems.* The old issues are neither dissolved by analysis nor reduced to settleable scientific questions. They survive the analytical process in a modified, transformed, more subtle and sophisticated form. They simply take on a reviewed and restored—if somewhat complicated—guise. Those patterns adapt, chameleon-like, to the conditions of the new conceptual environment.

(3) *The plasticity and flexibility of language.* The fluidity of our linguistic resources precludes the prospect of any single, unique, universal "analysis." The analytical process can improve no uniformity of problem resolution. The diversity of analytical alternatives comes to feature as part of the problem where philosophical issue resolution is concerned. Analysis is no royal road to the resolution of philosophical problems.

(4) *The deep disanalogy with science.* In natural science, the impact of experimentation upon theories blocks proliferation by eliminating alternatives. The observations we make in experimental situations serve to adjudicate conflicts in favor of some alternatives over others. With philosophical issues, by contrast, analysis simply highlights and fortifies disagreement and does not settle (dissolve or resolve) issues.

The overall upshot of such considerations is that logico-linguistic analysis, far from being a problem-resolving device provides a telescope that reveals the inescapable complexities in greater detail. The further the program was developed and extended, the less substantiation it provided for the doctrines it was designed to validate. Those traditional issues were not dissolved or resolved but instead reemerged in a more sophisticated, intricate and subtle forms. Analysis simply proves impotent as a problem-slayer and issue-resolver in philosophy.

What thus proved to be the undoing of the analytical enterprise was thus not a refuting criticism from without but an unraveling from within. As its adherents pressed the analytical program forward with ever intensifying dedication and energy, they were impelled into a range of findings that made a mockery of the program's initial motivating doctrinal commitments.

4. DEATH AND TRANSFIGURATION

As happens so often in the history of philosophy a programmatic vision was brought to grief not by external criticism but—ironically—through the contradictions brought to light through its internal development. Analytic philosophy did not die of old age but was laid low in its prime. And it was not killed off by its opponents; its demise was self-inflicted—in effect, the program committed suicide.

To be sure, either way the result is the same. Musing in 1990 on his earlier survey analytic philosophy, Richard Rorty writes: "The controversies which I discussed with such earnestness in 1965 already seemed quaint in 1975. By now (1990) they seem positively antique."[4] And Bernard Williams writes somewhat disdainfully of "linguistic analyis, that now distant philosophical style."[5] The philosophers of the 1990s are prepared to consign analytic philosophy to the history books and to move on to seek their philosophical inspirations elsewhere—not in logic and language but in history, in science, in the mathematics of computing and computers, in artificial intelligence, in literature, in Oriental mysticism, or whatever.

What does it mean for philosophy at large that analytic philosophy has faded from the Anglo-American academic stage where it only yesterday played so dominant a role? Does it mean a return to the status quo ante with business as usual and going back to things the way they were before?

By no means! For analytic philosophy has made a great difference and left a vast heritage.

The fact is that analytic philosophy has two substantially separable aspects. On the one hand, there is its doctrinal stance—its ideological vision of a post-philosophical era brought to realization by either dissolving or by reducing to empirical factuality the traditionary problems of the philosophical domain. This ideology was inherent in such procedural injunctions as: Do away with traditional philosophizing and use language-analysis to reduce philosophical issues to a scientific core—insofar as such analysis does not simply dissolve them altogether. Make use of them to endow the articulation and substantiation of your views with as much cogency and clarity as the circumstances of the situation admit of. All of this iconoclastic effort has indeed come to grief.

But the analytical project had another aspect. Apart from doctrine there were also method, technique, and modus operandi. This related to the program's methodological aspect which encompassed such procedural injunctions as: Strive to inject precision and clarity into your philosophical work. Do not be content with hazy ideas and unexamined assumptions but try to render your philosophical commitments as clear and explicit as possible. Develop and reform the instruments of logico-linguistic analysis and then make the maximal use of them to endow the activation and substantiation of your views with as much clarity and cogency as the circumstances of the situation admit.

The crucial consideration for present purposes is that (1) this *methodological* or procedural side of analytic philosophy is separable from its *ideological* or doctrinal side, and (2) that its influence is very much alive and continues at work all around us in the philosophical realm. In this respect analytic philosophy has made an ongoing contribution to philosophy in the Anglo-American setting (and well beyond). For its methodological sector has had a life of its own, apart from the doctrinal/ideological. And while analytic philosophy has made no lasting impact on the sorts of positions philosophers commonly hold, it has made an immense and lasting influence on the way in which they (or at any rate very many among them) do their work. Analytic philosophy's insistence on conceptual clarity and probative cogency—and the processes by which such desiderata are to be pursued—are factors that are very much alive and stirring on the contemporary philosophical scene. As a doctrinal program analytic philosophy has proved to be a dead end, a failure. But as a methodological resource it has proved itself immensely fertile and productive and its beneficial influence can be felt in every area of contemporary philosophy.

Even as the logical empiricism (or "logical positivism") of the interwar era died off, leaving in its wake an immensely fertile domain of history-and-philosophy of science (HPS), so the collapse of analytic philosophy has left in its wake a heritage of logico-linguistic sophistication that has transformed the way in which many academics nowadays do their work not only in philosophy but also in linguistics, historical studies, etc. Both of these philosophical positions—both logical positivism and the analytical movement—have enjoyed (or suffered) a very similar fate. In both cases we have seen the demise of the positive doctrinal program accompanied by the ongoing vivacity of an eminently productive methodological heritage.

And it is interesting to contemplate the future is this light. Insofar as the situation of analytic philosophy and logical empiricism may be seen as paradigmatic for ventures in "exact" philosophizing, this may foreshadow the fate that awaits the currently fashionable programs of "scientific" philosophy (based on the inspirations of artificial intelligence, computational theory, virtual reality, and the like). Here too we may plausibly expect an analogous course of developments, with such "movements" ultimately disappearing from the scene as viable doctrinal/ideological positions, but nevertheless leaving in the hands of working philosophers certain methodological instruments and intellectual resources that represent a permanent gain for the discipline.

Notes

1. The best account of the emergence and development of analytic philosophy is provided in the relevant chapters of John Passmore's excellent history, *A Hundred Years of Philosophy* (London: Duckworth: 1957). As this book began to circulate, Hegel's Owl of Minerva—that harbinger of academic mortality—was just commencing its overflight of analytic philosophy's domain.

2. For an informative survey see John Passmore, *Recent Philosophers* (La Salle: Open Court, 1985).

3. The logical positivists saw this clearly enough but drew the eminently problematic conclusion that the value domain should simply be sidelined as unsuited to rational deliberation.

4. Richard Rorty, *The Linguistic Turn: Essays—Philosophical Method—With Two Retrospective Essays* (Chicago: University of Chicago Press, 1992), p. 371. Rorty's book is still the best and most comprehensive anthology of the theory and practice of analytic philosophy.

5. Bernard Williams, "The Need to Be Sceptical," *Times Literary Supplement* (February 16-22, 1990), p. 163.

Chapter Three

ON WRITING PHILOSOPHY

OUTLINE

1. THE NATURE OF THE ENTERPRISE

Preliminaries

THIS discussion will offer some observations on the strategy, etiquette, and methodology of philosophical communication. It seeks to provide some critical and constructive guidance to writers of philosophy—and thus by indirection to readers as well. As the discussion itself will make all too clear, there is no intent here to provide dogmatic rules or impose any hard and fast distinction between what is acceptable and what is not, but only to offer some informal guidelines that can, so it is hoped, facilitate the job of the philosophical writer in reaching effectively such audience as fortune may provide.

The Task of Philosophy

Philosophy as traditionally conceived is the enterprise of using the resources of our reason to resolve, as best we can, the "big questions" regarding the nature of human beings and their place within the world's scheme of things. The history of philosophy consists in an ongoing intellectual struggle to develop ideas that render comprehensible the seemingly endless diversity and complexity that surrounds us on all sides. The instruments of philosophizing are concepts and theories—ideational structures—and it deploys them in quest of understanding, in the attempt to create an edifice of thought able to provide us with an intellectual home that affords a habitable thought-shelter in a complicated and challenging world.

The mission of philosophy is to ask, and to answer in a sensible and cognitively disciplined way, all those great questions about life in this world that people wonder about in their reflective moments. Aristotle was right on target when, in the first book of the *Metaphysics*, he said that "it is through wonder that men now begin and originally began to philosophize, wondering first about obvious perplexities, and then gradually proceeding to ask questions about the greater matters too, such as...the root origin of it all" (982b10).[1] Philosophy deals largely with *how*-and-*whether*-and-*why*-questions: how the world's arrangements stand in their relation to us, whether things are as they seem, and why things should be as they are (for example, why it is that we should do "the ethically right" things). Ever since Socrates pestered his fellow Athenians with puzzling questions about "obvious" facts regarding truth and justice, philosophers have probed for the reason why behind the reason why. What characterizes philosophy is its mission of grappling with "the big questions" of human concern:

- the place of humans in the world's scheme of things.

- the ways in which we ought to conduct our lives and our interpersonal affairs.

- how we should adjust our thoughts and actions vis à vis ourselves, our fellows, and the world around us.

And the method by which such inquiries are concluded in the orbit of philosophy as rational analysis, for what we seek are not just answers but rationally defensible and well-substantiated answers. Philosophy strives after that systematic integration of human knowledge which the sciences initially promised to give us but have never managed to deliver because of their ongoing division of labor and never-ending pursuit of ever more specialized detail.

Philosophy excludes no subject matter altogether. Its issues are too synoptic for the conscientious practitioner of the descriptive to rest content with any delimited range of preoccupation. For virtually *everything* is in some way relevant to its task of providing a sort of traveler's guidebook to the lay of the land in reality at large. Dealing with being and value in general—with possibility, actuality, significance, and worth—the concerns of philosophy are universal and all-embracing. The problem field of philosophy is as wide and borderless as is the domain of human knowledge itself. The reach of its concern is effectively unlimited—no issue in the dominion of nature or in the province of human thought is in principle outside its sphere of interest and concern or However, philosophy is neither natural science nor humanistic portraiture. What makes an issue philosophical is not the topic but the mode of treatment and the point of view from which the topic is considered. Philosophizing represents the product of people's attempts to bring intelligible order into our often chaotic experience of the world.

The Method of Philosophy: Truth-Estimative Conjecture

When philosophers pursue their mission of grappling with those traditional "big questions" regarding ourselves, the world, and our place within its scheme of things they standardly do so by means of what is perhaps best characterized as *rational conjecture*. And this is a tool for use by finite intelligence, providing them not with the best *possible* answer (in some rarified sense of this term), but with the best *available* answer—the putative optimum that one can manage to secure in the actually existing conditions in which we do and must conduct our epistemic labors. Rational conjecture is not to be a matter of *mere guesswork*, but one of *responsible estimation* in a strict sense of the term. It is not just some sort of estimate of the true answer that we want, but an estimate that is sensible and defensible—one to whose tenability we are prepared to commit ourselves. We have a need for more information than is strictly speaking in hand, but we certainly do not want to make it up "out of thin air." The approach of philosophy to its problematic concerns is as a branch of rational inquiry—a process of deploying our speculative abilities to seek out answers to questions that are validatable through cogent processes of evidence, inference, and the usual instruments of rational substantiation. However much speculation and conjecture may go into the process by which philosophers find their answers, evidence and argument must always pervade and underpin their presentation of them where *philosophizing* is at issue.

To be sure, in the information-deficient, conjecture-requiring circumstances that prevail when questions must be resolved in the face of evidential underdetermination, we can expect no logically airtight *guarantee* that what is, as best we can tell here and now, the "best available" answer is actually true. Given the information-transcendence at issue in philosophical truth-estimation, we know that we cannot guarantee the truth of its product. (Indeed, if the history of human inquiry has taught us any one thing, it is that the best estimate of the truth that we can make at any stage of the cognitive game will all too frequently come to be seen, with the wisdom of eventual hindsight, as being well off the mark.) Inquiry in philosophy, as elsewhere, is a matter of doing no more—but also no less—than the best we can manage to realize in its prevailing epistemic circumstances. Nevertheless, the fact remains that the rationally indicated answer does in fact afford our most promising *estimate* of the true answer—in the sense of that one for whose acceptance as true the optimal overall case be constructed with the instruments at hand.

The need for such an estimative approach to philosophy is

easy to see. After all, we humans live in a world not of our making where we have to do the best we can with the means at our disposal. We must recognize that there is no prospect of assessing the truth—or presumptive truth—of claims in this domain independently of the use of our imperfect mechanisms of inquiry and systematization. We are not—and presumably will never be—in a position to stake a totally secure claim to the definitive truth regarding those great issues of philosophical interest. But we certainly can—and indeed must—do the best we can to achieve a reasonable *estimate* of the truth. We can and do *aim* at the truth in our inquiries even in circumstances where we cannot make failproof pretentions to its attainment. We have no alternative but to settle for the *best available estimate* of the truth of the matter—that estimate for which the best case can be made out according to the appropriate standards of rational cogency. And *systematization* in the context of the available background information is nothing other than the process for making out this rationally best case. Accordingly, it is rational conjecture based on systematic considerations that is the key method of philosophical inquiry, affording our best prospect for obtaining sensible answers to the questions that confront us.

To be sure, the articulation thought framework that pervades awareness to philosophical questions is subject to individual perception and concern. The complexity and many-sidedness of the problem is such that there can be few—if any—general principles for their intelligent treatment. Human life and thought are so varied, so diversified, so many-sided in substance and interconnections that sensible discussions of the issues cannot be regimented by universalized specifications.

Are There Rules for Writing Philosophy?

There are no hard and fast rules for writing philosophy any more than there are hard and fast rules for writing poetry or history. Every philosopher must come to his or her own terms not only in substantive matters but also in dealing with the expository problems of the field. No one approach is fitted for every writer or suitable for all issues in philosophy. When addressing the issues, individual philosophers must attune their exposition to their own perspective—their own priorities and appraisals of the issues and bear upon them.

But although there are no *rules*, there certainly are *guide-*

lines–general norms that one is well advised to follow because in flouting them, one opens the door to avoidable problems and difficulties. Such guidelines are no more than mere "rules of thumb" that the teachings of experience indicate as deserving of respect. But to violate them without good cause is to invite yet further problems in a domain already strewn with difficulties.

Throughout the present discussion these strictures must be borne in mind. For wherever the discussion proceeds on the language of rules it must be understood that rules of thumb are at issue. And all such rules have their exceptions. Each one can be violated for good and sufficient reason, but such violations are never cost-free: each violation exacts some price, and one had best be sure that this is offset by some compensatory advantage. While the rules in this domain are mere guidelines and nothing hard and fast, one nevertheless violates them only at one's peril. Effective communication about philosophical issues is difficult enough that there is no point in making it harder for oneself than it needs to be.

The Audience

In writing philosophy, as in any other form of communication, the question of the nature of the audience is bound to arise. Is this to be one's fellow philosophers (the professors of the subject and their students), the general educated public, or that mysterious and as yet unpeopled realm of "posterity"?

Most likely, the best policy in this regard is indecision. Even when addressing professionals it is advantageous to be clear and explicit enough to be substantially accessible to students–at any rate in philosophy. And even when addressing students–or a substantially untrained public–it is best to try to be accurate and rigorous enough not to trouble the "experts." Moreover, the endeavor not to consign to unarticulated silence the presumptions and prejudices of one's age–exactly as though one were addressing posterity–is a useful merit in a philosopher.

Philosophizing is a work of reason and for reason. To whatever extent philosophical exposition can manage to address its issues with the intelligence with which all intelligent people deserve to be credited, a positive gain has been achieved. In philosophical exposition it is an undoubted merit to avoid particularizing the audience and at least to strive for universality of access–however imperfect the realization of this ideal will, in the end, prove itself to be.

2. DESIDERATA OF PHILOSOPHIZING

The Problem of Dialectics

Immanuel Kant tells us (quoting the Abbé Terrasson), that from the reader's point of view many a book would be shorter if it were not so short—if it provided more explanations, examples, clarifications. But while this is true enough, the balance of danger goes the other way. By and large, the risk that the philosophical author will try the reader's patience with excessive explanations and detail is greater than that the reader will be left wishing for a fuller exposition. (In general this is something that only book reviewers ask for, and not people who actually have to pay for the book.) Readers usually do not resent the challenge of having to figure something out for themselves.

After all, it lies in the very nature of philosophy that not all the i's can be dotted and the t's crossed. In principle every philosophical concept can be given further explanation, every philosophical thesis further substantiation. There is always more to be said. Each sentence can profitably use a commentary—and so can each sentence of that commentary. The answers we give to philosophical questions are always only rough and approximate. Our solutions to philosophical problems engender further problems. They are always open to challenges that require additional elaboration and refinement. In philosophy we are always impelled towards greater sophistication—our problem solving distinctions always bring yet further distinctions. We are led to compound wheels upon wheels—adding further epicycles of complexity to the theories we are seeking to render acceptable. The writer who insists upon completeness will wind up saying...nothing.

To be sure, one need seldom concede that a philosophical doctrine as such is inadequate, but only that its specific *formulation* in a particular "state of the art" is. The doctrine as a whole should be seen as a diachronic organism, something that develops and grows and changes over time, maintaining its identity not in its specific content but in its general orientation and, above all, in its genealogy—its exfoliative linkage to the core commitments from which it arose. A doctrinal position as such (i.e., in contrast to its specific formulation) is schematic, maintaining its identity through successive systemic formulations by its overall programmatic tendency rather than through its substantive detail.

We arrive at a model of philosophical development that is essentially exfoliative. Every philosophical position is linked to and developmentally derived from a prior doctrine that contains its root idea. (In the realm of philosophical thought as in physical nature we have *ex nihilo nihil*.) This exfoliative process involves a super engrafting of new distinctions upon old, with new topics and issues continually emerging from our efforts to resolve prior problems. There is an unending process of introducing further elaborative refinement into the setting of old, preestablished views, which sees an ongoing emergence of new positions to implement old doctrines. Thus, every philosophical concept and position always has a genealogy (an "archaeology," in currently fashionable terminology) that can trace back its origins programmatically through a means-end chain of problem solving. Every position and distinction has its natural place in the developmental tree.

No exposition of a philosophical position is ever long enough. Not theoretical adequacy but common sense alone can tell us when we have rendered a position of "enough said."

Clarity

Philosophical positions are large, complex, elaborate structures. They do not neatly lend themselves to condensation, abbreviation, summarizing. All the same, the philosopher who does not have an accessible message—who does not present a compactly summarizable answer to an identifiable question—is asking for trouble. For philosophy must, in the end, be bound up with the problems and issues of life, with people's ventures at coming to intellectual and practical terms with themselves, their fellows, and the world. The philosophers whose deliberations cannot readily be brought into a discernible explanatory relationship with these issues run a real risk that people will consign their efforts to the storage shelves of material defunct in relevancy and interest. To address those whose interest is geared to the remote technicalities is to run a real risk of confining one's readership to this sparsely populated group. If one has something of value to say it is well worthwhile to make the effort to gain for it the widest practicable audience.

Our philosophical questions are always answered incompletely, in ways that inevitably leave further crucial detail to be supplied. And in fact in recent times philosophy has moved toward increasing technicality and sophistication. So much so that it makes interested bystanders impatient. They cry, "Will philosophy ever again address the heavens? Will it contribute anything to man's vision, rather than merely clarifying it?"[2] But this sort of complaint overlooks the filiation of means and ends in question resolution that links the technical issues of philosophy to the fundamental presystemic questions from which they arise. We are (or should be!) driven to those technical microissues by the inexorable necessity of addressing them in order to secure rationally adequate resolutions of the presystemic macroissues afforded by "eternal problems" of philosophy.

A happy medium between over- and underexplaining has to be struck in philosophical writing as elsewhere. And here we must set out from the basic consideration that in philosophy nothing can be explained completely—all the way down. Enough must be said to remove ambiguities and possible misinterpretations. But the trouble with excessive detail is that it tends to lose sight of the issues and to introduce misleading emphases. (In this regard it is worth contrasting the essays of G. E. Moore with those of Bertrand Russell.) To be sure, the adequate treatment of technicalities is sometimes unavoidable, and technicalities require detail. The writer who does not use good judgment in this may soon lose those readers, however, once the reader becomes persuaded that the effort-to-return ratio for those technical elaborations is turning unfavorable.

After all, total clarity is never attainable in philosophy. The philosopher is caught in the bind created by two facts. (1) No concrete philosophical statement is ever adequate to the issues: every philosophical statement needs further commentary and explanation—more delineation and qualification. (2) No philosophical statement is altogether clear until its full explanation is provided. It is an inexorable consequence of these facts that we can never get clear but only clearer. The best one can do in philosophical matters is to provide what clarity suffices for our present purposes. And it is easy to make errors here. Writers know (or *think* they know) what they want to say. But it is easy to misjudge how matters look from where the reader stands. Still, one does well to try for as much clarity as one can afford to obtain within the limits of the available space and time. For insofar as we are not clear, we defeat our own communicative purposes. Since we write to convey and convince, unclarity inevitably puts obstacles in the way of our aims.

Philosophy is, after all, a matter of publicly accessible inquiry.

The basic problems with which philosophers deal are public property, so that the inquiries have to be conducted in the public domain by means of generally available conceptual resources. If thinkers did not see these doctrines and supporting arguments as public objects—communally available and appraisable—they would be doing something very different from *philosophizing*.

Admittedly, clarity is not enough. But when other things are anything like equal, it is greatly preferable to its contrary. The writer who makes obscurity a trademark does well to have an unalloyed confidence in the quality of his work. For in making their writings obscure philosophers take a step in the direction of condemning them to obscurity.

Maintaining Touch with a Tradition

To all intents and purposes, philosophers fall into groupings that are internally united by an affinity of doctrinal fundamentals, but externally divided from one another in distinct "schools of thought" and "traditions." On the surface, it certainly seems to be a fact of life that there are always different schools of philosophical thought regarding "the same" issues—different approaches to resolving "the same" problems. Philosophers seem usually to belong to warring tribes. In antiquity we have Aristotelians and Platonists, Stoics and Epicureans; in the middle ages, Thomists and Augustinians and Scotists; in modern times Rationalists and Empiricists, and so on. Or so it seems. But various theorists have recently argued that these appearances are misleading. What seem to be conflicting philosophical doctrines are in fact—so they contend—totally separate positions that are actually incomparable or incommensurable. Such discordant positions—so these incommensurability theorists maintain—simply cannot be brought into contact with one another; they be compared in point of agreement or contradiction because no common measure of comparison can be established between them. Different philosophers do not, in fact, form schools that hold divergent views on "essentially the same issues"—they actually share no issues and live in disjoint cognitive domains that share no common territory. Rival doctrinal positions are totally disconnected; different theories are incommensurable—they cannot be expressed in common units of thought. Adherents of different theories literally live in different thought worlds, among which contact—be it by way of disagreement or agreement—is simply impossible.

In the English-language orbit, the prime spokesman for such a view was R. G. Collingwood:

> If there were a permanent problem P, we could ask "What did Kant, or Leibniz, or Berkeley, think about P?" and if that question could be answered, we could then go on to ask "Was Kant, or Leibniz, or Berkeley, right in what he thought about P?" But what is thought to be a permanent problem P is really a number of transitory problems, P_1, P_2, P_3,...whose individual peculiarities are blurred by the historical myopia of the person who lumps them together under the name P.[3]

Various intellectual historians share this point of view, maintaining that every thinker stands alone—that every teaching is ultimately distinctive, every thesis so impregnated with the characteristic thought style of its proponent that no two thinkers ever discuss "the same" proposition.

On such a view, there just are no "schools of thought" constituted by different thinkers who share common commitments and no "perennial issues" treated in common by successive generations of theorists. Different thinkers occupy different thought worlds. Disagreement—indeed even comprehension—across doctrinal divides becomes impossible: the thought of every thinker stands apart in splendid isolation. Discordant philosophers can never be said to contribute to the same ongoing issues: "There are simply no perennial problems in philosophy: there are only individual answers to individual questions, with as many different answers as there are questions, and as many different questions as there are questioners."[4] Philosophers of different persuasions are separated from each other by an unbridgeable gulf of mutual incomprehension. So argue the theorists of doctrinal incommensurability.

The fact, however, is that this view exaggerates mutual incomprehension to the point of absurdity. Of course, incomprehension *can* and sometimes *does* occur across reaches of time or space when major conceptual dissimilarities are involved. But this is certainly not the case generally or necessarily.

There is, after all, no shortage of examples of problems and issues discussed by different philosophers working in different times and places. Protagorean relativism, Cartesian scepticism, Berkeleyan phenomenalism are all issues that our contemporaries can identify and examine equally well as their inaugurators—and accept or reject in whole or in part as their own commitments would indicate. Philosophical concepts and issues can certainly be transposed from one systematic setting to another, despite any differences of nuance and attunement derived from their particular context of origin. Indeed even the very question that we are presently discussing ("Can Different Philosophers Debate the Same Issues?") is a clear-cut example of this commonality of issues, with, for example, Collingwood and Randall assuming essentially the same holistic position and the present discussion rejecting it—along with the entire doxographic tradition. To insist that deliberations about the nature and function of the law in St. Thomas Aquinas are incommensurable with those in Kant is like saying that the Alps and the Rockies cannot both be mountain ranges because they are so different.

To deny the possibility of philosophical disagreement on grounds of incommensurability is to abandon the enterprise as a meaningful cognitive project from the very outset. Only if disagreement is possible does the enterprise make sense. Philosophical positions have a point only insofar as they *deny* something: *omnis affirmatio est negatio.* They claim truth by denying falsity; they assert saving insight by attacking dangerous error. To this end there must be contrasts. If one denies the very existence of rival positions and views them as literally *inconceivable,* there can be nothing substantial to one's own view. Where there is no opposition to attack, there is no position to defend. To see rival positions as incomprehensible is to demean and devalue one's own; if opposing positions were conceptually ungraspable in their very natures, there would be little use in taking a stance that precludes them. Where no possible rival position has the least plausibility, advocacy of a particular doctrine as the "appropriate" position becomes altogether pointless.

Without the prospect of shared problems and theses considered in common by diverse thinkers, all hope of interpretation and comprehension is lost. Every thinker—indeed each one of us—would be locked within the impenetrable walls of his own thought world. If one philosophical mind cannot connect with another, then *we* ourselves cannot connect with anyone either. In the absence of relatability to other times and places, the historian himself would be faced with issues that he is incapable of dealing with. If Kant cannot address Hume's problems, neither can Collingwood. If conceptual contact across the divide of conflicting beliefs were impossible, then, given the diversity of their views, all philosophers would be condemned to mutual incomprehension. Were it the case that, as a matter of principle, X would not come to grips with a rival theorist Y by way of agreement or disagreement, then we ourselves would be condemned to philosophical solipsism—unable to come to make a rational assessment of the ideas of any other thinker due to an inability to make conceptual contact. If philosophers cannot speak to one another, then they cannot speak to us either. Any prospect of communal discussion of shared issues is at once destroyed. If the conflicting views of philosophers cannot be brought into touch—if they indeed are strictly incommensurable, with each theory enclosed in a world of its own—then they become altogether inaccessible. We all become windowless Leibnizian monads—though bereft of the coordinative benefit of a preestablished harmony.

A dogmatic insistence on cognitive incommensurability is unprofitable and self-defeating. Contact of *some* sort among philosophical doctrines is essential. Determinists and indeterminists do not generally disagree about what causality is, but about its pervasiveness. Sceptics and cognitivists need not disagree about the idea of knowledge, but about its availability. Statists and libertarians do not clash about what desires individuals have, but about the weight these should carry in public policy deliberations. All such controversies flow from agreement about the range of jurisdiction or desirability of certain factors with respect to whose *nature* there is little or no disagreement. If we cannot in principle relate the thought of distinct philosophers by way of identity and similarity, if we cannot say that here they are discussing the same (or similar) questions and that there they are offering consonant (or conflicting) answers, then we shall be in bad straits indeed. For if we cannot relate X's thought to Y's, we cannot relate it to *ours* either. We are locked into mutual incomprehension. (And worse; what makes for so great difference between X's understanding of Y and X's understanding of the X of a year ago who also held rather different opinions? A cognitive solipsism of the present moment looms.)

In writing philosophy we have no sensible alternative but to proceed on the supposition that others can understand us in the sense we intend—if they are willing to make a sufficient effort which we are well advised to make as undemanding as possible. And we do well to explain, develop, and substantiate our own position in terms of its relationships with the ideas and doctrines to which it is linked by way of affinity or opposition.

To be sure, this can be overdue. Philosophical writers frequently indulge negative explanations. Employing formulas like "In saying thus I don't mean to maintain so," they are telling us about what they do *not* claim or believe or assert in a well-intentioned endeavor to head off misunderstanding. But they often seem insufficiently aware of how unproductive this can be. Guarding against misinterpretation is all very well, but the range of things one may *not* mean is usually so large that it is not particularly enlightening to be presented with a few items that can safely be stricken from the list. It is perhaps more painful for the author, but certainly more helpful to a reader when writers take the *via positiva* and set out, plainly and explicitly, what they are prepared to assert. Authors who have not thought things through to the point of feeling comfortable about accentuating the positive have apparently not yet managed to develop their ideas to a point where they merit the exposure of publication.

Heeding the Guidance of Logic

Few features are more advantageous to a philosophical discussion than the maintenance of a logical order of exposition that renders the filiation of ideas and the relationship of theses as clear and conspicuous as possible.

But Descartes' fond vision to the contrary notwithstanding, the presentation of a philosophical position generally does not easily lend itself to the linear mode of exposition of pure mathematics, moving from axiomatic first principles to ever more complex derivative truths. The realm of fact and reality just does not have the neat sequential structure of written exposition. A philosophical exposition must be logical: it must present its ideas in a rational and coherent way. But this does not mean that it will exhibit a predestined sequential order, proceeding along an inexorable line of development from a starting point in unavoidable first principles. In giving an account of the nature of things, philosophers must impose a certain rational order on the materials at issue—exactly as with those who set out to provide an account of a city or of a country. And—within limits—they are free to do this in many different ways.

Moreover, philosophical problems frequently make demands of their own. Often they will not allow one to work in the way one would prefer, but insist that the discussion proceed in *their* way. And when this occurs, there is no use struggling against the inevitable.

A philosophical position, like a defended city, will have some sectors more weakly protected than others. The writer of philosophical deliberations can be quite sure that readers will probe for such weak spots—to say nothing of referees and reviewers. One is well advised to take preventive measures to bolster them in advance—enlisting the aid of friends and colleagues insofar as possible. No position is totally vulnerable against objection, but there is no point in making things more difficult for oneself than necessary. In philosophy, perhaps more than in any other mode of writing, criticism is a boon—provided it comes before rather than after publication. Of course, philosophical excellence is not a matter of tight reasoning alone—or even primarily. But loose thinking certainly does not advance its cause.

Philosophy does not furnish us with new ground-level facts; it endeavors to systematize, harmonize, and coordinate the old into coherent structures in whose terms we can meaningfully address our larger questions. The prime mover of philosophizing is the urge to systemic adequacy—to achieving consistency, coherence, and rational order within the framework of what we accept. Its work is a matter of the *disciplining* of our cognitive commitments in order to make overall sense of them—to render them harmonious and coherent. Two prime injunctions regarding the mission of rational inquiry accordingly set the stage for sensible philosophizing.

(1) Answer the questions! Say enough to satisfy your curiosity about things.

(2) Keep your commitments consistent! Don't say so much that some of your contentions are in conflict with others.

To be sure, there is a tension between these two imperatives—between the factors of commitment and consistency. We find ourselves in the discomfiting situation of cognitive conflict, with different tendencies of thought pulling in divergent directions. The task is to make sense of our discordant cognitive commitments and to impart coherence and unity to them insofar as possible.

Note that a writer's claims do not wear their reasons for acceptance on their sleeves. Few and far between is the sentence able at one and the same time to state a claim and to present explicitly the reason for its acceptance—to make an assertion and at the same time to offer a reason for accepting it. After all, even a claim of the form "*P*—and moreover *O*, which is the case, constitutes a good reason for accepting *P*" still leaves open the question: "But why accept *O*?" Claims do not—nay, generally cannot—be self-validating in concurrently presenting the grounds for their own acceptance. What they achieve is not to *state* the grounds for their acceptability, but at best to *suggest* them to the perceptive reader.

And here, once again, the writer is well advised to be helpful to readers. For cogent legitimation is the indispensable requisite of philosophical adequacy. And where this is not forthcoming readers have no right to be satisfied and authors no right to ask for our endorsement of the views at issue.

It is this aspect of philosophical exposition that marks the disceptive as a venture in rational inquiry. No matter how pretty the story, or no matter how much it appeals to our imagination or our admiration—however much it enlists our approval—it can make no claims on our *understanding* save through the instrumentality of reason.

Setting the Stage

Philosophical authors like to start *in medias res*; they want to get straight into the issues and ventilate their views on their chosen topic. They have made the problem their own—have read up on it, been fascinated by it, become deeply involved with it. And having (one hopes) grappled the issue for some time, an author finds it all too easy to lose sight of the fact that readers will approach the discussion in a less prepared state of mind. Philosophers find it difficult to bring themselves to believe that something so central and significant to themselves is generally not comparably crucial for others—that the great mass of their readers are not equally concerned and interested, let alone informed and prepared.

Unfortunately, here, as elsewhere, our readers may not look at things as we ourselves do. There is a job of stagesetting and motivation to be done—of *salesmanship* to put it bluntly. This is a task that philosophical authors neglect at their own peril.

Three questions are crucial at the outset: (1) Just what is at issue—what is the problem being addressed? (2) Whence does it arise, how did it come to figure on the philosophical agenda?

(3) What hinges on it, what patently philosophical concerns are so intimately connected with these deliberations that they can make a real difference in the larger scheme of things?

Most philosophical authors find such preliminary stagesetting bothersome. They want to jump right in and get on with it. But it is neither reasonable nor prudent to leave this sort of thing as "an exercise for the reader." The reader, alas, has many other demands on his time and attention and may well elect to channel these resources in other directions.

3. ISSUES OF TECHNIQUE

References

One interesting aspect of philosophical discussions lies in their references to other contributions to their subject—or lack thereof. Most basically, the following cross-classification should be brought to bear in this connection:

- mere mentions *vs.* actual discussion

- favorable *vs.* critical stance: substantiative *vs.* refutatory mention

A good deal of information can be obtained about the tendency and position of a philosophical publication simply by knowing this sort of thing about the authors discussed or cited.

Referential analysis can lead to interesting typological groupings. Some authors refer only to opponents, others only to congeners. Some writers refer solely to the great dead. (A. N. Whitehead would break this rule only for personal friends.) Others refer only to contemporaries, or sometimes only to countrymen. Even writers on justice often do not trouble to do justice to those of their fellow theorists to whom they are indebted.

The philosophical literature has unquestionably become too large in recent years to permit anything like a general survey of discussions relevant to most significant problems. But surely the author who simply makes no real effort in this direction is delinquent. In particular, if he avoids any mention of the sources of his inspiration, he is an ingrate (if not worse). And in general one becomes hung on the horns of a dilemma in neglecting "the literature." If one is simply unaware of relevant discussions, then one's professional competence is called into question. If one deliberately omits mention of relevant discussions because they are not written by members of one's own school or group, then one betrays pettiness and provincialism. All such failings betoken a regrettable betrayal of sound standards. In philosophy parochialism is even less excusable than elsewhere.

Philosophy too has its nonpersons. The natural habitat of academic nonpersons is in the spaces between footnotes; they are prominent through their absence. Like the servants in an old-world mansion, they are part of the unnoticed background, victims to the pretense that they do not exist at all. We sense they are there, but do not hear from them. However useful their contribution, it is made in unnoticed silence.

Nonpersons are not born but made. We create them. Sometimes through defects in knowledge. ("Ignorance, madam, sheer ignorance.") Sometimes through parochialism. How easily those of another language, tradition, or school slide into nonpersonhood! (Think not, gentle reader, that intellectuals are any less likely to slide into "us" *versus* "them" thinking than the great unread.) And sometimes we create nonpersons through sheer snobbery. Who wants to acknowledge concern with—let alone indebtedness to—thinkers of whom "our crowd" will not think all that well?

To be sure, one cannot take note of everything written in a highly active field of research. But one should at least make some effort to keep in touch with the literature—and to acknowledge what did come to notice. Often, writers seem to deem the roster of their citations as a kind of social register. Only the great and good whom we would think of inviting to our house for a party are to be found there—others are untouchables who must be excluded with care. "Heaven forfend that the pages of my paper or my book should be defiled through mention of X's discussion of the issue!" Nonpersons, alas, are made not born. We create nonpersons through lack of information, impartiality, or urbanity.

Yet this sort of thing is literally irresponsible. Authors on scholarly subjects surely have a responsibility to inform our readers not just about their own views but about the state of the art. Of course, we are free to criticize what we mention, or even to dismiss it with scorn. But simply to ignore a substantially relevant contribution is, however understandable, nevertheless inexcusable. It is accordingly a salutary and illuminating exercise for philosophical authors who think a paper (or book) that they are working to be completed to take up the manuscript once more, and carry out a referential analysis to see if what has in fact been done in this regard reflects the actual intentions at work.

Problematic Silences

A philosopher's silences can be pregnant with interest. They may, of course, simply reflect conceptual inaccessibilities: Aristotle could obviously not discuss the philosophical ramifications of quantum theory. ("Whereof one cannot speak thereof one must be silent.") Then, too, they may merely betoken a want of time or of information. But they may also indicate something more weighty—an overt decision to ignore, a judgment of unimportance, an explicit dismissal of concern.

What can excuse silence? Well, for one thing, a theory on which there is nothing viable (true, appropriate) to be said on the topic at issue. Examples are afforded by the view positivists take of metaphysics, or again by the position of sceptics towards philosophical doctrines in general. But from the true philosopher one would expect not mere silence but explanation. Why should it be that an issue is unimportant, why should it be seen as uninteresting, or why should it be deemed worthy of dismissal? The philosopher as philosopher owes us an account. In philosophizing there can be errors of omission as well as errors of commission; not only can a philosopher's claims be wrong but his silences can be inappropriate. Not only can we disagree with what a philosopher says, but we can reproach him or her for discreditable silences as well.

In this light, consider the situation of women. Feminist historians of philosophy provide constant reminders of the extent to which philosophers from Plato and Aristotle onwards have cast aspersions on women. But there are notable exceptions, although, prior to J. S. Mill, they generally manifest themselves rather by silence than explicit argumentation. An example is Leibniz who on a personal plane held various women in high esteem in point of intellectual capacity, and who was in any case too astute a courtier to articulate views that would be offensive to the several highnesses with whom he dealt on a daily basis. When such writers discuss persons without bringing women explicitly into the discussion it is presumably not because they dismiss the gender *en gros* but because they see it as self-evident that their remarks about people in general pertain to men and women indifferently.

On Avoiding Undue Technicalities

Nonphilosophers sometimes ask, "Why is so much present-day philosophical writing boring and irrelevant?" A substantial divide apparently separates the issues that intrigue philosophers themselves from those which nonphilosophers think that philosophers ought to discuss. The principal reason why the nonspecialist obtains this impression is that contemporary philosophical writing is in great measure technical and addressed to the specialist alone. But why should this be? Is it perhaps simply a matter of the fashion of the day? By no means! There is good reason for it. Contemporary philosophers generally do—and surely always should—deal with technical issues in the field because they are *constrained* to do so. They address this technical issue to resolve another in order to resolve yet another and so on until finally one reaches the point of what is needed to resolve some probably significant presystematic, nontechnical issue.

A thread of means-ends filiation should always link philosophical technicalities to the nontechnical "big issues" of life, the universe, and everything with which philosophy traditionally deals. Philosophical technicalities can be unavoidable means to sensible ends—and should, in fact, only be there when this is so. They matter when—but *only* when—they are required for the satisfactory handling of something nontechnical. Regrettably, however, people sometimes become entranced by technicalities for their own sake. They are unwilling to take the time and trouble to explain to their colleagues (let alone to laymen) why those technicalities matter, how they arise out of the fundamental issues of the field, and why they are needed to resolve problems satisfactorily. They talk—and want to talk—only with fellow specialists, fellow technicians whose concern for technical issues can be taken for granted. And then those complaints about irrelevancy will clearly be placed. The cardinal principle is that technicalities should be minimized: they should never be multiplied *praeter necessitatem* but only be resorted to insofar as necessary. It is true that technicalities may become unavoidable in the adequate treatment of philosophical issues, but it is also no less true that they should never be deployed beyond the point where they indeed are unavoidably required.

A considerable host of philosophers from Hume to Russell and beyond show that it is possible to do both technical philosophy and popular communication—occasionally even in one and the same book. Unfortunately, too few philosophical writers are willing to make the effort.

On Avoiding Historical Caution

More than any other family of academic researchers, philosophers are constantly harking back to the work of their predecessors. They are imbued with the fear of being accused of reinventing the wheel or rediscovering the North Pole. But constantly looking back over one's shoulder is not only likely to give one a stiff neck, it also makes it hard to be forward-looking.

From Socrates onwards, there are encouraging precedents for creative work in philosophy with only modest attention to the burdens of the past. And there is something to be said for such an approach. If we are too fearful of doing injustice to the past, we shall have to preoccupy ourselves with it to an extent that makes it hard to get on with the work of the present. If we become too heavily burdened with the freight of the books of bygone thinkers, we shall lack the time and the energy to think for ourselves. Unable to get on with our proper task, we shall become becalmed—with various colleagues and some entire university departments—in the sterile waters of ancestor worship.

The philosopher who is unduly afraid of making *wrong* claims, of making mistakes, is in grave difficulty through an excess of caution. But so is the philosopher who is overly afraid of making *anticipated* claims, of making repetitions. The former is condemned to scepticism, to saying nothing. The latter is condemned to retreating into history, to rehearsing what has been done to the detriment of creative innovation. He is in danger of joining those for whom, in Kant's words, "the history of philosophy becomes a substitute for philosophy itself."

Every generation must do its own philosophical work, must find its own answers to the "big questions" that crowd in upon it from many sides. If it can find help ready-made in the labors of bygone days, that's just splendid. But this is eminently improbable. The history of philosophy can be a useful tool for philosophical work. But historical studies are no substitute for philosophizing.

The retreat into history-mongering and the withdrawal into scepticism both represent a comparable failure of nerve in philosophizing, an unwillingness to take the cognitive tasks of the day into hand in the face of the difficulties and risks that are inherent in the enterprise.

On Avoiding Self-Reference

Descartes placed the "I" front and center on the philosophical stage. In fact, as he saw it, it is only by the grace of God that we get from there to anywhere else. Berkeley deemed the whole world a collection of I's. They call to each other across the matterless void like coyotes howling across an empty plain. Throughout philosophy, the I is of good repute and thorough respectability. Metaphysics would miss it sorely. Philosophical psychology would be stymied without it. Its absence would leave a great void in epistemology. But *stylistically* the matter stands on a very different footing. Here an I omitted is a merit gained.

Philosophical writers, alas, are all too fond of the first person. As a quick glance at the journal literature soon substantiates, contemporary philosophers are addicted to avowals: "I shall try to show," "I think that it is clear," "It seems strange to me that," and a myriad of such self-referential locutions pervade the writings of our colleagues. Indulgence in self-reference has become one of the banes of contemporary philosophical exposition. "I find this unintelligible." "I find it difficult to see how X gets from A to B." "I think one must agree that...." One is tempted to respond: "Do tell us more about yourself, you sound interesting." After all, I-assertions are inevitably personal avowals. But if something is indeed obscure or true—or the reverse—an author can surely tell us so without bringing himself into it. He is ostensibly discussing an issue, not writing an autobiography. The writer who says "It is unclear to me" to mean "It is unclear" is not only guilty of undue verbosity but is being pointlessly egocentric about it.

First-person avowals, of course, say nothing about the issues: whatever claims they make relate to the state of the author's mind and not to substantive question. To address an issue one must make a statement, rather than presenting an attitudinal or intentional avowal. To place that cat one must *assert* "The cat is on the mat"; it will not do to state that X says so or that Y thinks so (oneself included). Avowals, clearly, are autobiographical and not substantive instrumentalities.

Where did the modern philosopher catch this I-itis? Perhaps from G. E. Moore—that master of self-reference. (The opening paragraph of "Is Time Real?"—admittedly an uncommonly long one—contains thirty-three I's, with six of them in that most dispensable of all contexts, "I think.") Perhaps the matter stood rather differently in the era of G. E. Moore and William James. In that heyday of academic pomposity, their chatty use of the first-person pronoun had a certain unpretentious charm evocative of faculty club informality. It carried a useful message: "Let's not do philosophy by pretending to speak *ex cathedra* in the name of the World Spirit. Let's stop being Herr Professor, and admit we're speaking for ourselves, not for the universe." But times change.

To address an issue one must make a statement, rather than presenting a personal avowal. To place that cat one must *assert* "The cat is on the mat"; it will not do to state that X says so or that Y thinks so (oneself included). Avowals, clearly, are autobiographical and not substantive instrumentalities. Rare is the philosophical point that cannot be made without bringing oneself into it.

4. ISSUES OF PROBATIVE AUTHORITY

Data and Claims to Conviction

When writing philosophy it is always advantageous to bear in mind how the situation looks from the reader's point of view. In particular, the writer of philosophy should constantly be asking: Just why is it that the reader should accept this claim of mine? And shrewd readers will also bear this in mind, constantly asking themselves—sentence by sentence just why the author claims should be accepted. With philosophical discussions, the reader can and should engage in a constant dialogue with the text, at each step challenging it with the question: On what sort of basis can the author expect us to accept the assertion at issue? Is it as a matter of scientific fact, of common sense—of "what everybody should realize"—of accepting the assertion of some expert or authority, of drawing a suitable conclusion from previously established facts, or just what? In reading—or writing—a philosophical discussion one is well advised to step back from the text and consider the prospects of such a legitimation-commentary.

Ultimately, the issue of acceptability is always one of considerations we are expected to endorse or concede because of the plausibility of their *credentials*. And this has many ramifications.

Be it as single individuals or as entire generations, we always start our inquiries with the benefit of a diversified cognitive heritage, falling heir to that great mass of information and misinformation that is the "accumulated wisdom" of our predecessors—or those among them to whom we choose to listen. What William James called our "funded experience" of the world's ways—of its nature and our place within it—constitutes the *data* at philosophy's disposal in its endeavor to accomplish its question-resolving work. These "data" of philosophy include:

(1) Common-sense beliefs, common knowledge, and what have been "the ordinary convictions of the plain man" since time immemorial;

(2) The facts (or purported facts) afforded by the science of the day; the views of well-informed experts and authorities;

(3) The lessons we derive from our experiential dealings with the world in everyday life;

(4) The received opinions that constitute the world-view of the day; views that accord with the "spirit of the times" and the ambient convictions characteristic of one's cultural heritage;

(5) Tradition, inherited lore, and the transmitted wisdom of the past;

(6) The "teachings of history" as best we can discern them.

No plausible source of information about how matters stand in the world fails to bring grist to philosophy's mill. The whole range of the (purportedly) established "facts of experience" furnishes the extra-philosophical inputs for our philosophizing—the materials, as it were, for our philosophical reflections.

All such philosophical data deserve respect: common sense, tradition, general belief, accepted (i.e., well-established) prior theorizing—the sum total of the different sectors of "our experience." They are all plausible, exerting some degree of cognitive pressure and having some claim upon us. They may not constitute irrefutably established knowledge, but nevertheless they do have some degree of merit and, given our cognitive situation, it would be very convenient if they turned out to be true. The philosopher cannot simply turn his back on these data without further ado.

Still, even considering all this, there is nothing sacred and sacrosanct about the data. For, taken as a whole, the data are too much for tenability—collectively they run into conflicts and contradictions. The long and short of it is that the data of philosophy constitute a plethora of fact (or purported fact) so ample as to threaten to sink any ship that carries so heavy a cargo. Those data are by no means unproblematic. The constraint they put upon us is not peremptory and absolute—they do not represent certainties to which we must cling at all costs. What we owe to these data, in the final analysis not *acceptance* but merely *respect*. In philosophizing even the plainest of "plain facts" can be questioned, as indeed some of them must be. For what counts here is, in the final analysis, not our individual beliefs but the entire belief system as a whole. The mission of the enterprise is, after all, to make sure of things across the board, not only to get answers, but to have them be coherent and systematically harmonious.

Argumentation and Rhetoric in Philosophical Method

There are two very different modes of writing philosophy. The one pivots on inferential expressions such as "because," "since," "therefore," "has the consequence that," "and so cannot," "must accordingly," and the like. The other bristles with adjectives of approbation or disapproval—"evident," "sensible," "untenable," "absurd," "inappropriate," "unscientific," and comparable adverbs like "obviously," "foolishly," etc. The former relies primarily on inference and argumentation to substantiate its claims, the latter primarily on the rhetoric of persuasion. The one seeks to secure the reader's (or auditor's) assent by inference and reasoning, the other by an appeal to values.

Consider the following passage from Nietzsche's *Genealogy of Morals* (with characterizations of approbation/derogation indicated by italics):

> It is in the sphere of contracts and legal obligations that the moral universe of guilt, conscience, and duty (*"sacred" duty*) took on its inception. Those beginnings were *liberally sprinkled with blood*, as are the beginnings of *everything great on earth*. (And may we not say that ethics has never lost its *reek of blood* and torture—not even in Kant, whose categorical imperative *smacks of cruelty?*) It was then that the *sinister knitting together* of the two ideas guilt and pain first occurred, which by now have become quite inextricable. Let us ask once more: in what sense could pain constitute repayment of a debt? In the sense that to make someone suffer was *a supreme pleasure.* To

> behold suffering gives pleasure, but to cause another to suffer affords an *even greater pleasure*. This *severe statement* expresses an old, powerful, *human, all too human sentiment*—though the monkeys too might endorse it, for it is reported that they heralded and preluded man in the devising of *bizarre cruelties*. There is no feast without cruelty, as man's entire history attests. Punishment, too, has its *festive features*. (Friedrich Nietzsche, *The Geneology of Morals*, Essay II, Sect. 6.)

This passage is replete with rhetorical devices of an evaluative tendency. But observe too the total absence of inferential expressions. We are, clearly, *invited* to draw certain unstated evaluative conclusions. But the governing inference "Man is by nature drawn to and pleased by cruelty, and so cruelty—being a natural and congenial inclination of ours—is not something bad, not something that deserves condemnation" is left wholly implicit; it is hinted at but never stated. In consequence, one can gain no fulcrum for pressing the plausible objection: "And why should something to which we are drawn automatically be therefore good: why should the appeal of a sentiment or mode of behavior safeguard it against a negative evaluation?" By leaving the reader to his own conclusion-drawing devices, Nietzsche relieves himself of the labor of argumentation. By avoiding explicitness in stating his conclusion, he feels no need to give it overt *support*; he is quite content to *insinuate* it.

In contrast to the preceding Nietzsche passage, consider the following ideologically kindred passage from Hume's *Treatise* (with the evaluative terms italicized and inferential terms capitalized):

> Now, SINCE the distinguishing impressions by which moral good or evil is known are nothing but particular pains or pleasures, IT FOLLOWS that in all inquiries concerning these moral distinctions IT WILL BE SUFFICIENT TO SHOW the principles which make us feel a satisfaction or uneasiness from the survey of any character, IN ORDER TO SATISFY US WHY the character is *laudable* or *blamable*. An action, or sentiment, or character, is *virtuous* or *vicious*; WHY? BECAUSE its view causes a pleasure or uneasiness of a particular kind. In giving a reason, THEREFORE, for the pleasure or uneasiness, we sufficiently explain the vice or virtue. To have the sense of virtue is nothing but to feel a satisfaction of a particular kind from the contemplation of a character. The very feeling constitutes our praise or admiration. We go no further, nor do we inquire into the cause of the satisfaction. WE DO NOT INFER a character to be *virtu-*

ous BECAUSE it pleases; but in feeling that it pleases after such a particular manner we in effect feel that it is *virtuous*. The case is the same as in our judgments concerning all kinds of beauty, and tastes, and sensations. Our approbation is IMPLIED in the immediate pleasure they convey to us. (David Hume, *Treatise of Human Nature*, Bk. III, Pt. I, Sect. 2.)

While for Nietzsche cruelty is effectively a virtue because (so it would seem) people are held to be statistically pleased by engaging in its practice, for Hume it is something negative only in that people are held to be statistically displeased by witnessing it. The positions differ but their ideological kinship is clear: both writers agree that cruelty is not something that is inherently bad as such but that such normative status as it has depends on the statistics of people's reactions and attitudes.

What is also clear, however, is that these kindred positions are advanced in very different ways. In the passage from Nietzsche, the "argumentation ratio" of inferential to evaluative expressions is zero, in the Hume passage it is quite high. Hume, in effect, seeks to *reason* his readers into agreement; Nietzsche to *coax* them into endorsing it.

Reflection on the contrast between the argumentative and the rhetorical modes of philosophical exposition leads to the realization that these two styles are attuned to rather different objectives. The demonstrative/argumentative (inferential) mode is efficient for securing a reader's assent to certain claims, to influencing one's *beliefs*. The rhetorical (evocative) mode is optimal for inducing a reader to adopt certain preferences, to shaping or influencing one's *priorities and evaluations*.

The argumentative, *apodictic* (or probative) mode of philosophical exposition is by nature geared to a view of philosophy that sees the discipline in *information-oriented* terms, as preoccupied with the answering of certain questions: the solution of certain cognitive problems. It aims primarily to *convince* by way of inferential reasoning.

By contrast, the rhetorical, *prohairetic* (or preferential) mode of philosophical exposition is by nature geared to securing acceptance with respect to *evaluations*: to enlisting the reader's agreement to certain priorities or appraisals. It is preoccupied with evaluation, with forming—or reforming—our sensibilities with respect to the value or preferability of the items at issue. It is bound up with a view of philosophy that sees the discipline in *axiological* terms, as an enterprise that aims at securing certain evaluative determinations and the establishment of certain prizings, approbations, and priorities. It seeks primarily to entice people to share an evaluative standpoint—proceeding not by inferential reasoning but by inducing the reader to see the handwriting on the wall.[5] This rhetorical approach comes into its own by enabling an exposition to appeal to—and if need be reconfigure—a reader's body of experiences in order to induce a suitable alignment of evaluations. There are, of course, many ways to achieve this sort of objective. A display of suitably related case studies, a survey of selected historical episodes ("History teaching by examples"), or even a vividly articulated fiction can orient a reader's evaluative sentiments in a preplanned direction, particularly when supplemented by a suitably tendentious interpretative exegesis. The assembling of illustrative materials—real or constructed—can render good service in this regard, as the example-surveying philosophical methodology of Ludwig Wittgenstein amply illustrates. And so, of course, can pure invective, if sufficiently clever in its articulation; witness Nietzsche.

Two distinct views of the mission of the enterprise are at issue with the demonstrative (rationality) and evaluative (rhetorical) approaches to philosophy. For this reason, the primary dispute over the respective merits of the two modes of philosophical exposition is inseparable from a dispute about the nature of philosophy. The quarrel is ultimately one of ownership: to whom does the discipline of philosophy properly belong—to the argumentative demonstrators or to the evaluative charmers?

This contest over the ownership of philosophy has been going on since the very inception of the subject. Among the Presocratics, the Milesians founded a "nature philosophy" addressed primarily at issues we would nowadays classify as explanatorily scientific, while such thinkers as Xenophanes, Heraclitus, and Pythagoras took an evaluative approach to philosophy—illustrated by the following dictum of the last-named:

> Life is like a festival; just as some come to the festival to compete, some to ply their trade, but the best people come as spectators, so in life slavish men go hunting for fame or gain, the philosophers for the truth. (Frag. 278, Kirk & Raven.)

In nineteenth-century German philosophy, Hegel and his school typified the scientific/demonstrative approach, while the so-called "irrationalists" who were their principal opponents—Schopenhauer, Kierkegaard, Nietzsche—all exemplify the axiological/rhetorical approach. In the twentieth century, the scientistic movement represented by logical positivism vociferously insisted upon the methodology of demonstration, while their anti-rationalistic opponents among the existentialists and also among the neo-Romantic theoreticians of Spain (preeminently including Unamuno and Ortega y Gasset) resorted extensively to pre-dominantly literary devices to promulgate their views—to such an extent that their demonstration-minded opponents sought to exile their work from philosophy into literature, journalism, or some such less "serious" mode of intellectual endeavor.

But the irony is that philosophers simply cannot dispense altogether with the methodology they reject and despise. Even the most demonstration-minded philosopher cannot altogether escape entanglement in evaluation by rhetorical devices. For one cannot argue inferentially for everything, "all the way down," so to speak. At some point one must invite assent through an evaluative appeal that marshals those "data of philosophy" to one's own ends. On the other hand, even the most evaluation-minded philosopher cannot altogether avert argumentation. For a reliance on certain *standards* of assessment is inescapably present in those proffered evaluations, and this issue of appropriateness cannot be addressed satisfactorily without some recourse to reasons.

Ironically then, the two modes of philosophizing are locked into an uneasy but indissoluble union. Neither the inferential nor the evocative side can feel altogether comfortable about using the methodology favored by the other, and yet neither side can manage to get on altogether without it.

Philosophical Interpretation

Like all other humans, philosophical writers are flawed and imperfect beings. From the standpoint of even the most sympathetic of readers, their discussions can all too often be seen as committing errors of various sorts.

For one thing, there are errors of omission. As such, these are ambiguous. They may betoken mere disinterest or, somewhat more drastically, an explicit (albeit usually unexpressed) intention to dismiss a certain matter as uninteresting or unimportant. But silence may also result from the inaccessibility of certain concepts in particular culture-contexts—as Aristotle could not have considered the philosophical implications of quantum theory.

Then too there are those even more striking errors of commission. These are mistakes in reasoning—in thinking erroneously that one can get from here to there—often from innocuous premises to striking conclusions. Even worse are outright inconsistencies—of asserting on page 12 what one denies on page 92, or of endorsing premises that engender conclusions one denies. Few and far between are the authors who, in dealing with complex issues, affirm many things over many pages while managing to avoid lapses of this kind.

All the same, these harsh realities notwithstanding, systematicity is the expository ideal in philosophical exposition. Ideally, at its theoretical best, the philosophical treatment of an issue should be coherent, consistent, complete, connected—a unified and systematic whole.

And this fact underlies the Golden Rule of philosophical interpretation: in interpreting the discussions of a philosopher, do all you reasonably can to render them coherent and systematic. The operative principle is one of charity, as it were: do unto another as you would ideally do for yourself.

The interpretation of philosophical texts is accordingly a procedure with a definite methodology of its own. It combines in interactive symbiosis a commitment to two prime desiderata:

- faithfulness to the text.

- commitment to establishing the coherence, consistency, integrity—and, in sum, the systematic viability—of the ideas at issue.

On this basis, faced with alternative, textually viable interpretations, that one is *ipso facto* the superior which renders the author's thought more systematic—more effective in resolving the philosophical problems that are at stake in the text's discussion.

Another aspect of this situation is that the *burden of proof* always inclines against the critic. The writer who claims to find inadequacies in the text—who charges its author with inconsequence in the development of ideas, and incompetence of lack of consistency, coherence, etc.—always has a heavy burden to discharge. For the salient interpretative presumption is that the author is competent and to defeat this presumption it does not suffice that there is *some* potentially viable interpretation that sustains the objections at issue, but rather that there is *no* viable interpretation that defeats them. And universal theses are notoriously more difficult to substantiate than particular ones.

The complexities of philosophical interpretation—and its inherent room for slack created by inductive variation—means that definitive perfection is unachievable in this domain. This creates major burdens for the philosophical writer, who has no choice but to place a substantial return on the readers' goodwill. (To be sure this should never be abused—or ever stretched beyond current limits.) And it also raises problems for philosophical readers who are confronted with the point of alternative interpretations.

The range of conflict can often be reduced by considerations of context. For we can find guidance regarding the evaluative matters at issue from other texts of the author's, from other authors of his time and place, from wider ancillary information about the envisioning society and culture, etc. Accordingly these interpretative matters can lead well beyond the confines of the *text* itself to enhance an almost endlessly variegated range of *contextual* considerations.

With an ever-broadening body of peripheral scholarship, the domain of context becomes ever-widening, so it is somewhere between unlikely and impossible that a final definitive interpretation of substantial and complex philosophical texts can ever be achieved. But the rules of the game are perfectly clear:

- "Save the phenomena" of text and context insofar as possible.

- Be charitable: always give the author the benefit of doubt. Try insofar as possible to provide a substantive interpretation that preserves the coherence, consistency, unity, etc., of the position at issue—in short, that makes the philosophical discussion at issue as systematic as possible.

Yet what happens when these two desiderata come into conflict?

We here arrive at the distinction between the *philological* interpreter and the *philosophical* interpreter. For the former, the first item has the priority. "In your reconstructive efforts, focus upon text and context and let doctrine look after itself." But with the philosophical interpreter, the priorities are reversed: "In your reconstructive efforts, endeavor to provide for a systematic doctrine—one that is adequate to the philosophical problems and thus informative, coherent, consistent, etc."

The philosophical interpreter can never neglect the work of the philologists, which is, after all, essential for understanding the text and the context that are crucial to the project. But, nevertheless, the priorities of the philosophical interpreter lie elsewhere—with the *philosophical* rather than the merely *textual* side of the interpretative problem.

5. ISSUES OF QUALITY

Producing Rubbish

The media of philosophical publication—books, monographs, journals—are, unintentionally to be sure, in the business of producing ephemera. For within a year or two after its appearance, most of this material is gathering dust on shelves, never to be perused again. Like rubbish in general, it is ready for the scrap heap. Much of this rubbish is not even like a worn-out razor blade—useful in its prime although now no longer functional. Nor is it like an old automobile—presently obsolete but fraught with potential for revival as a classic. It is more like a soup can or a candy wrapper—something we initially have no choice but to accept and yet later throw away in order to be able to get at the good stuff with which it came. To be sure, such intellectual discard-packaging differs from the real thing in that nobody ever sets out deliberately to produce it as such. Authors fondly imagine they are creating first-rate material; editors fondly imagine they are publishing it. But in the end, things just do not quite work out that way.

We can no more abolish rubbish in our publications than we can do so in our households. For in philosophy telling rubbish from the prime goods is more difficult than we would like. This is so for two reasons.

The first is that in philosophical inquiry the determination of excellence is generally a matter of *hindsight*. In many cases, we can only tell rubbish from good stuff retrospectively with the wisdom of posterior information at our disposal. We have to see where ideas lead to and what can be made of them to determine their merit. The utilitarian theory of evaluation by consequences may have its defects in ethics, but it has much to be said for it in the sphere of philosophizing where the fruitfulness and usefulness of ideas is a major factor.[6]

The second reason is that discriminating rubbish from the good stuff is also a matter of *wholesight*. For we have to see how ideas fit into the wider context of relevant thought to understand their full significance and to make a realistic appraisal of their value. To see the interest, value, and tenability of a philosophical idea we have to consider it not in isolation but as part of a bigger picture. F. H. Bradley was an important thinker not so much because of his peculiar argument for the irreality of time and of relations, but because of the important insights into the substance of Hegelian thought that his work provides. In philosophy, the line between crank and genius can be hard to draw precisely because issues of development and context—of hindsight and wholesight—are pivotal.

To a large extent, rubbish is unavoidable in philosophy. Its presence is an unavoidable part of the *sine qua non* conditions for obtaining the good stuff. Telling philosophical writers not to produce rubbish or philosophical editors not to publish it is like telling oil prospectors not to drill dry holes or farmers not to plant crops in inauspicious seasons. For in all such matters we lack effective foresight. In philosophy, one cannot tell where dead ends are until they have been created, inspected, explored and reflected on. As in supermarket shopping, accepting rubbish is an unavoidable part of bringing home the bacon. To be sure, this is not an argument against having standards. It is, rather, an insistence on recognizing that there are definite limits to what even the best of standards can do for one in this domain. Though to say this is obviously not to deny that it is worthwhile to make every effort to reduce rubbish as much as possible by doing what one plausibly can. This leads to the topic of—

Peer Review

In editorial selection, as in all modes of quality control, there are two kinds of errors. Errors of the first kind relate to rejected items that should have been accepted; those of the second kind relate to accepted items that should have been rejected. Readers generally deem editors as particularly liable to errors of the second kind, authors incline to see them as prone of errors of the first kind. The editors themselves think they get it just right—until the material is in print and they turn into readers.

When book publishers meet, conversation frequently dwells on egregious errors of the first kind—"the big ones that got away," those manuscripts one declined that subsequently proved outstandingly successful for another house. As best I can tell, this doesn't happen very much with the editors of philosophy journals. Work that actually is outstandingly meritorious is so rare that its loss is not a worrisomely frequent experience.

To minimize errors, editors generally recruit outside help. Basically, there are three alternatives. In the interests of quality control, editors can rely on their own judgment (across the board?)—as Gilbert Ryle was reputed to do during his administration of *Mind*. Alternatively, the editor can rely on the judgment of the authors ("This is a great article I'm sending you"—or, as somebody once told me in a follow-up telephone call, "I've really worked hard on this one"!). Or the editor can take the route of peer review and rely on the opinions of third parties who (as best one can tell) have some degree of expertise and good judgment in the area at issue. No system is perfect, none avoids errors totally. Certainly not peer review—for that peer is only human and doubtless has a full share of lapses and human failings (in addition to a particular philosophical point of view). It's all a matter of percentage and proportion. Peer review is a thoroughly imperfect system, the alternatives to which are even worse.

Philosophobia

But if given up on the idea of these being absolute and unproblematic standards of merit in philosophy, perhaps one should abandon the entire enterprise?

We are living in a time of *post*-periodization. People tell us that our economy is post-industrial (even though more gadgets are being produced than ever, largely by robots). Our philosophy is characterized as postmodern (even though to the historian of modern thought much of its substance seems *déjà vu*). Philosophical expositors and theorists are nowadays fast on the draw with labels like *post-metaphysical* or *post-epistemological* —even though working metaphysicians and epistemologists whose name is legion seem never to have got the word.

What a handy resort, this post-ing business is! If you find a tendency of thought or an area of theorizing uncongenial, you need not bother to examine and criticize it in detail—with one swift swipe of the tarring bush of *post*-characterization you consign its entire genre to the trash heap of what is outmoded, passé, and just plain not with it. How convenient a way of trashing what we dislike!

What we have here is a popular theme of modern thought— the idea that intellectual history is not a matter of continuity and evolutionary development that allows tendencies of thought the benefit of revisionary adaptations in the face of changed circumstances, but rather is a succession of abrupt revolutionary shifts that leave major tendencies of thought beyond the prospect of renovation, adjustment, and transformation. Descartes' new turn mindwards, Kant's idea of a new "critical," post-metaphysical era in philosophy, or Auguste Comte's conception of a new scientific era that readers null and void all earlier programs of theological and metaphysical thought, are only some prime examples of doctrines that claim such abrupt discontinuities—as is the Nietzschean conception of a postmoral age. How ever-tempting is this idea of a totally new dawning that liberates us once and for all from a concern for the reflective labors of the past. And yet how deeply problematic!

The idea that substantial alternatives in philosophy can somehow fall off the edge of the world is a comforting illusion. It is, after all, very convenient to dismiss doctrines as obsolete— for then we no longer have to take the trouble to figure out exactly what it is that renders them untenable (or at any rate unacceptable to us). But invariably these supposedly all-transforming revolutions run their course only to see the old conceptions rise phoenix-like from the ashes in a duly refurbished form! How convenient it is in the midst of an information glut to have a plausible excuse for not troubling our minds about various sorts of issues! How we yearn for an excuse not to read (let alone think!) about various ideas, theories, and doctrines. And yet how wrong this is in philosophy where all substantial positions have unextinguishable life in them. How easy and yet futile it is to issue death-certificates in philosophy!

And this is particularly so with respect to philosophy itself. Throughout the long history of this subject there have been schools of thought antipathetic to philosophizing and urging the abandonment of this endeavor. From classical antiquity onwards, the *sceptics* have maintained the impotence and incapacity of reason. Those "big questions," so they insist, simply lie beyond the reach of reason, placed outside the range of questions that human reason can answer. Philosophy's attempt to resolve them is inescapably futile. In an analogous way, the *sophists* always maintained that while reason can indeed provide answers to these questions, it will provide too many of them. An equally cogent case can be made out from each and every one of various alternative answers. What reason cannot do is to *decide* between them, no one of them admitting of a justificatory case any stronger than that for the others. Again, in more recent days *logical positivism*, and deconstructionism as well, maintain that the questions are inherently meaningless. The reason why we cannot resolve them lies not in limitations of human reason but in the inherent senselessness of the issues. The questions at issue are inherently flawed though involving literally meaningless terms (logical positivism) or false presuppositions (Kant) or mistaken preconceptions ("postmodernism" or deconstructionism). Again, positivistic *scientism* (or *scientific positivism*) insists on reducing or transforming the traditional big questions into orthodox scientific issues. It is not that the questions are intractable but rather that when their sense is appropriately understood—duly analyzed and "clarified"—they reduce to scientific issues of the familiar sort. When science has done its work, there is no residual work left for philosophy. Finally, *historicism* insists that at this stage, there is no work left for philosophy itself because the residual work should be accomplished—not by *science*, but—by *history*. At this time and in this era we should not address philosophical issues directly by taking them at face value, but rather should see the issues in an altogether historical light. The appropriate course consists in surveying the history of philosophical theorizing of all sorts. For philosophy itself we can and should substitute the history of philosophical theories and ideas.

Each of these very different doctrinal positions agrees that philosophy as traditionally conceived should be abandoned, and that something very different (or perhaps only a vacuum) should take its place. All of these positions propose to abolish philosophy in anything like the form that has characterized the traditional mainstream of the subject.

What is striking about all these positions, however, is their self-inconsistency—the fact that each of them violates its own prescriptions. The sceptic is not sceptical about the correctness of his own position. The sophist does not think the positions that rival his own are equally meritorious. The deconstructionist does not regard his own strictures against philosophy as ultimately meaningless. Adherents of scientism are clearly unable to characterize the issue of philosophy's possibility as itself somehow representing a scientific question. And, finally, the historicist is not prepared to replace his own position with discussions exclusively devoted to a noncommittal survey of what

ON WRITING PHILOSOPHY / 79

people have thought and said about this topic. To be consistent with our situation and with our place in the world's scheme of things, we humans have little alternative but to philosophize—if not on our own, then via the good offices of others in whose footsteps we are content to tread.

The ironic fact is that all of these philosophy-rejecting doctrinal positions come to grief through the selfsame circumstance that *metaphilosophy*—the consideration of the nature, scope and methods of philosophy—is an integral part of philosophy itself. Any critical examination of the scope and merits of philosophy will itself form part of the philosophical venture at large. Given this circumstances, it is clear that even these who try in a reasoned way to maintain and substantiate that philosophy is not possible are thereby engaged—self-defeatingly—on a project of philosophical investigation. To engage in rational argumentation designed to establish the impossibility of philosophizing is actually to be engaged in doing a bit of it. We can, in the end, refrain from reading and writing philosophy, but not philosophizing is harder to excuse. And to do this well, it helps to interchange ideas with others—that is, to read and write about the issues of the field. Communication—the exchange and criticism of ideas—is the very lifeblood of philosophizing. As long as such communication is done competently and conscientiously, the philosophical author has nothing to apologize for.

The fact is that we humans have a very real and material stake in securing viable answers to our questions about how things stand in the world we live in. In situations of cognitive frustration and bafflement we cannot function effectively as the sort of creature nature has compelled us to become. Confusion and ignorance—even in such "remote" and "abstruse" matters as those with which philosophy deals—yield psychic dismay and discomfort. The old saying is perfectly true: philosophy bakes no bread. But it is also no less true that man does not live by bread alone. The physical side of our nature that impels us to eat, drink, and be merry is just one of its sides. *Homo sapiens* requires nourishment for the mind as urgently as nourishment for the body. We seek knowledge not only because we wish, but because we must. For us humans, the need for information, for knowledge to nourish the mind, is every bit as critical as the need for food to nourish the body. Cognitive vacuity or dissonance is as distressing to us as hunger or pain. We want and need our cognitive commitments to comprise an intelligible story, to give a comprehensive and coherent account of things. Bafflement and ignorance—to give suspensions of judgment the somewhat harsher name they deserve—exact a substantial price from us. The quest for cognitive orientation in a difficult world represents a deeply practical requisite for us. That basic demand for information and understanding presses in upon us and we must do (and are pragmatically justified in doing) what is needed for its satisfaction. For us, cognition is the most practical of matters. Knowledge itself fulfills an acute practical need. And this is where philosophy comes in, in its attempt to grapple with our basic cognitive concerns and our deep-rooted commitment to those "big questions."

The question "Should people philosophize?" accordingly receives a straightforward answer. The impetus to philosophy lies in our very nature as rational inquirers: as beings who have questions, demand answers, and want these answers to be as cogent as the circumstances allow. Cognitive problems arise when matters fail to meet our expectations, and the expectation of rational order is the most fundamental of them all. The fact is simply that we must philosophize; it is a situational imperative for a rational creature such as ourselves. Writing philosophy—especially *good* philosophy—is undoubtedly strugglesome work, but somebody has got to do it.[7]

Notes

1. Oxford translation (modified). Actually, Plato's Socrates already maintained that wondering (*thamazein*) is the root-source (*archē*) of philosophy (*Theaetetus,* 155d).

2. Essay: "What (If Anything) to Expect from Today's Philosophers," *Time,* January 7, 1966, p. 25.

3. R. G. Collingwood, *An Autobiography* (Oxford: Clarendon Press, 1939), p. 69.

4. J. H. Randall, *The Career of Philosophy,* Vol. 1 (New York: Columbia University Press, 1962), p. 50.

5. The issue here is not one of *reason vs. evaluation*; both demonstration and evaluation are perfectly good rational processes.

6. In utilitarian ethics, we must shift from actual to predictively presumptive consequences, but in inquiry there is unfortunately no secure avenue to such prediction.

7. Some of the material of this chapter is drawn from the editorials that the author has contributed to the *American Philosophical Quarterly* over the years.

Chapter Four

OBLIGATION DYNAMICS AND DEONTIC METAMORPHOSIS

1. PROBLEMS OF OBLIGATION DISCHARGE

SOME obligations are assumed voluntarily, such as those inherent in the responsibilities of a captain for the safety of the passengers or a babysitter for the children in question. Other obligations come our way through circumstances beyond our control, such as the obligation to thank the random passerby who has pushed us out of harm's way on a busy street. Either way, obligations and duties are an integral part of the moral domain in which we humans live, move, and have our being.

But this world is a harsh environment not of our own making. All too often, uncooperative circumstance prevents us from discharging various obligations. It is thus clear that obligations can issue in a variety of results. For one thing, they can come to an end, either by being met, honored, discharged; or else by being failed, dishonored, violated. However, they can also lapse from efficacy by way of metamorphosis—by not being honored and yet staying in force in a changed way, through being altered by circumstance into some other form. It is this phenomenon that will preoccupy us here.

Consider an example. You borrow $5 from Smith, to be repaid on a certain day. As the time nears, you collect the money together, but en route to the settlement you are robbed of everything you have down to $4. Thanks to unavoidable circumstances beyond your control, you now cannot honor that initial obligation to repay in full. But it is clearly not "lost without trace." Other obligations come to stand in its place—along the lines of: "To offer Smith an explanation and an apology; to pay him what you can manage now, and to repay the rest as soon as you conveniently can." Again, you promise your friend Jones, who seeks employment, to help him in his job search by introducing him to your Uncle Robert, who owns a factory that is hiring employees. But as the time approaches, your uncle dies of food poisoning and you yourself inherit the firm. That original obligation is now unfulfillable as such. But it is clearly succeeded by an obligation on your own part to look for a post in the factory for Jones. Such examples substantiate a larger point. In general, when uncooperative circumstance renders it impossible to discharge an obligation as it stands, a successor obligation that is derivative from it comes to stand in its place.

Sometimes our moral obligations can even derive from the defaults of other people. If you observe that the blind beggar drops some money and his seeing companion unaccountably ignores the situation, the duty to help is incumbent upon you, like it or not. You borrow Smith's lawnmower. You are killed in an auto accident. Your wife as heir now also inherits the moral—and not *merely* legal—obligation to return that mower to Smith. On the other hand, suppose that you had also promised Jones to help tutor his son in algebra. That obligation dies with you, seeing that such services are not transmissible through inheritance in the way material goods are.

When we acknowledge (as we must) that "circumstances" can contravene the discharge of an obligation, we have to recognize that they can do so in two very different sorts of ways. On the one hand, they can render an obligation's discharge *impossible*. (You promise to meet John at a certain place and time. John is killed in an auto accident en route.) On the other hand, they can render this discharge *inadvisable*—that is, *morally* impracticable. (You promise to meet John at a certain place and time, but have to miss the appointment in order to administer first aid to an injured stranger you meet along the way.) Some moral obligations are clearly overridden by others of even greater weight. Obligations that become impossible to honor may or may not leave derivative successors behind, depending on the circumstances. But *overridden* obligations will always do so. For in all such cases, there will be new obligations to explain, apologize, compensate, etc. A transmutation takes place—a metamorphosis.

2. Obligation Metamorphosis

Undischargeable and overridden obligations can change their form. Consider an example. You promise to help Smith clean out his garage next weekend. As the time approaches you are rushed to the emergency room with a broken arm. This unhappy development renders the original obligation unmeetable. But it does not thereby destroy it through a cancellation into a nothingness where it is lost without trace. Rather, it changes or transforms it, for it is now metamorphosed into an obligation to offer Smith help at a future juncture. What the agent is now obliged to do differs, but the force of the original obligation persists to exert itself upon a somewhat different object. The original obligation remains—not, to be sure, exactly as was, but in a transformed version. What I *am* obliged to do differs from but is nevertheless grounded in what I *was* obliged to do. (Note that the new obligation, albeit emergent from the original one, is not in any sense a *part* of it, and is thus better described as *derivative* rather than as *residual*.)

How obligations metamorphose is also affected by the existence of other obligations. You owe $5 to Smith and also $5 to Jones. The day before payment is due you are robbed of everything, down to $8. You can pay the one or the other (in full)—but not both. Given the symmetry of the two cases, it seems appropriate that each debtor is now due a payment of $4—along with inevitable explanation, apologies, and assurances for the future.

There are very different routes to the infeasibility of discharging a moral obligation. Thus the impossibility of carrying out some duty may be due to "fate" or may result from one's own deliberate contrivance, and from a moral point of view this makes all the difference. You promise to give your neighbor a lift to his brother's house on your way to the airport for a business trip that you are taking. Your boss calls, informing you that the trip is cancelled. End of obligation. But suppose you promised to join the group helping your neighbor to raise his barn next Saturday. That morning you become drunk as a lord and couldn't even raise yourself to an upright position, let alone help with the barn. A very different situation now prevails. Insofar as *ought* implies *can, can not* implies *need not*. But these are very different rules to commit, and their moral bearing is very different.

The question whether one sees the successor to a circumstantially unrealizable obligation as being a new *replacement for* a now-defunct old obligation or rather as a circumstantially forced *transformation of* an old, ongoing obligation may seem more or less "academic"—a mere matter of style, of mode of formulation. But there is a significant *theoretical* difference. If the original obligation simply expired, thereby losing its entire deontic force through a complete lapse from existence, no obligatoriness would remain to pass on to its metamorphosed successor version—whose status as a valid duty is, after all, totally derived from it. But this just does not appear to be the case. The question of whence it is that the later obligation derives its deontic force is thus far more easily and directly answerable on the transformation than on the replacement account. On the transformation account the old obligation *persists* in a new, metamorphosed form. While on the replacement account the old obligation *expires* and a new successor mysteriously springs up in its place. But in no other context do we find things to spring out of existence to be followed by conveniently adjusted new successors popping up to take their place. We long ago gave up such occasionalism in mechanics and in metaphysics, and there is no cogent reason for retaining it in ethics either.

On such a transformative approach, obligation is regarded as a rather different point of view, construed not so much as discrete items but as complex ongoing processes that change and adapt themselves to changing conditions. In short, we arrive at *a process view of obligation*.

It is tempting to think of an obligation as consisting simply and wholly in a duty to perform a specific particular action, "to pay $5 to John." But this is quite wrong. Even which is at issue with something so simple as "Paying $5 to John on or before 5 February" is not just a particular action but actually a vast assemblage of possible actions. And an instruction on the lines of "to pay $5 to John if that is possible but if not then to pay it to his heirs" does not of itself characterize *actions* at all, but something much more complicated. (Though even this is not complicated enough to do justice to the actual situation, which also contemplates the prospect of various sorts of inabilities to pay.) The fact is that obligations are almost infinitely complex—they *involve* particular actions all right, but generally only in extremely convoluted ways. They are, in sum, rather intricate processes of action-management—too complex in nature to be captured by any single readily formulable instruction regarding concrete courses of action.

3. OUGHT IMPLIES CAN?

It is far from clear that we *can* do everything that we ought (morally) to do. We *ought* to forget old wrongs, to rejoice at the good fortune of people we dislike, to forgive our enemies. Yet it is questionable that we actually can do so—except perhaps in the trivial sense of *logical* possibility. Psychologically—perhaps even physiologically—this sort of thing may be more than we can bring ourselves to do. Given the realities of our situation we just might not be able to manage it. But that of course does not get us off the hook of that *ought*.

Suppose you take little Johnny to the zoo. You are careless, and little Johnny is reckless. He sticks his leg into lemur's cage and the critter bites him. Johnny cries and to calm him down you promise to make it stop hurting soon. But you cannot actually do so; anesthesia—let alone a magic wand—just is not available. We have an apory:

- *Ought* implies *can*: whatever you ought to do you actually can do.

- You ought to keep your promises.

- You promised Johnny to make it stop hurting.

- You cannot make it stop hurting.

The four statements are inconsistent. One of them has to be abandoned—or modified. The last being a "fact of life," we get a choice between the first three.

One could drop the third, subject to the idea that no actual promise was made by you in uttering those soothing words because a *genuine* promise exists only where its fulfillment is indeed possible. (No doubt you ought not to have made that unkeepable promise—and perhaps that very fact stops the putative promise from being a real one.) This approach represents a convenient but highly implausible principle. Promises can be forced into default by unforeseen future contingencies. But surely the issue of *making* a promise is independent of whether this promise *will*—or even in the light of later unforeseeable developments *can*—be kept.

Again, one could, perhaps, drop the second thesis, taking refuge in the idea that it properly ought to read:

"You ought to keep your promises if (but only insofar as) it is possible for you actually to do so."

If we take this line of cutting the *ought* (rather than the *promise* itself) back to what ultimately proves to be feasible, then we do indeed save "ought" implies "can"—but only by way of the trivializing equation, *ought = ought insofar as you can*, which, its *ad hoc* character apart, is, all too clearly, very dubious. (After all, getting oneself into a fix where doing so becomes infeasible does not necessarily terminate one's obligation to keep a promise.)

The least problematic course is—to all appearances—to dispense with that first thesis, and reject "ought" implies "can" at the level of unqualified generality.

Consider the following situation. You borrow $100 from Smith, promising to return it at a certain designated time. You have (only just) sufficient funds to repay Smith, and near the appointed hour you are en route to Smith's house to do so. But on the way there you are mugged and the money is stolen. Seemingly we have a clash:

- *Ought* implies *can*.

- You ought to repay Smith.

- You cannot repay Smith.

Again the last statement of this inconsistent triad is simply a "fact of life"—so we have to choose between the first two in our effort to obtain consistency. We could thus proceed either by replacing the first statement with

- *Ought* ought to carry *can* in its wake—but sometimes it just does not.

or by replacing the second with

- You ought to repay Smith—but only insofar as you can actually manage to do so.

But clearly the second route to consistency restitution is deeply problematic, as was already noted above. The first alternative is clearly our best available option.

There is no doubt that "ought" *ought* to imply "can." But in the real world it unfortunately does not do so. "Every person willing and able to work *ought* to have a job." Right—no question about it. But whether they all *can* do depends on the state of the economy. "Everyone *ought* to have enough to eat." True. But whether we all *can* do so depends on how many of us there are on the planet. Clearly an *ought* does not in general suffice to assure a *can*. This is simply an unpredictable fact of life that we have to come to terms with.

It lies in the logic of the situation that "ought" implies "can" will obtain iff "cannot" implies "need not"—that is iff incapacity annihilates obligation. And this it surely does not do in any automatic, across the board way. For here the crucial question is: What is the nature of that incapacity. How did it come into existence?

If "ought" invariably implied "can"—if infeasibility *automatically* curtailed obligation—then there would be an incongruity —an actual inner inconsistency—to saying:

> "He ought to be mindful of that infirm pedestrian crossing the road in front of his car, but he just cannot, being too drunk."

But there is clearly no inconsistency here.

The sentry on duty cannot challenge the intruder because he has drugged himself into sensibility; the soldier cannot join his mates in the attack because he has shot himself in the foot; the debtor cannot repay the debt because he has gambled the money away. It is clear that in such cases where an incapacity is self-generated for reasons of one's own conveniences and wishes, no one would say that the agent's obligations have been annihilated through this fact. We would surely say something like: "The agent ought even now to be performing these actions, although—regrettably and quite wrongly—he has put himself into a position of not being able to do so." "You ought to honor your obligations" is not automatically tantamount to "You ought to honor your obligations insofar as the circumstances allow," because we are entitled to go on to inquire why it is that you find yourself in those fulfillment-inhibiting circumstances. Incapacity does not automatically render an obligation null and void.

Only the most inordinately lenient among us would restructure the obligation claim at issue to readjust it to what the agent actually can do. Various situations of infeasibility are such that an obligation remains operative, the agent's default notwithstanding. And ordinary language recognizes this fact by adding the special marker "by rights" to indicate the extraordinary character of the situation: "Smith ought by rights to repay Jones, although he regrettably cannot, seeing that he has gambled the money away." In this formulation we *qualify* "Smith ought to repay Jones" but certainly do not *abandon* it.

As such considerations indicate, it is advisable to distinguish in this context between ordinary/normal and extraordinary/abnormal situations. In *ordinary* cases, "ought" does indeed imply "can." But in (sufficiently) extraordinary cases "ought" can actually coexist with "cannot"—as the example of the drunken sentry illustrates. For while the ordinary sorts of "cannot" conditions (namely, externally generated incapacities) would indeed get our sentry off the hook of obligation, that extraordinary self-inflicted incapacity just does not do the trick. The "ought"-implies-"can" principle does not hold hard and fast—all across the board. It obtains *automatically only* with regard to *normal* and *ordinary* cases. The ethical principle of "ought" implies "can" is thus yet another illustration of a philosophical generalization that does not hold in a strictly universally and absolutely exceptionless way, but only obtains standardistically, allowing certain sorts of literally extraordinary exception cases to slip through its net.

And so while *ought* does not imply *can* unqualifiedly, it would be unproblematically appropriate to say that it does imply *"can if all goes well."* That is, if even under the most favorable circumstances and conditions there is no feasible way of discharging a putative obligation, then that "obligation" is dissolved as such. But the unqualified thesis must be abandoned.

It is precisely because your "oughts" depend largely on yourself—or commitments that you have assumed voluntarily—whereas your "cans" (your abilities to perform on the day) depend largely on circumstances beyond your control that a gap opens up between obligation and capacity that makes room for deontic metamorphosis. It is when circumstances beyond one's control prevent one from doing what under *normal* and *ordinary* conditions one ought to do that obligation dynamics comes into play to transmute those original obligations into a form and condition adapted to the new circumstances. And in particular, when the infeasibility of discharging an obligation is a matter of an agent's own deliberate contrivance, then the agent is morally reprehensible and all sorts of derived obligations (to explain, to apologize, to provide moral and even material compensation) spring into being.

4. PRINCIPLES OF OBLIGATION MANAGEMENT

This introduces the theme of *conflicts* of obligation. Obligations do not conflict *in abstracto* but in their competition for the allocation of the same resources—time, money, etc. The time I promise to spend with you I cannot also dedicate to another. The money or fealty I owe to X I cannot also bestow upon Y.

Now if I promise to spend all day this Saturday helping Smith to clean out his attic and also promise to help Jones to clean out his garage, I have placed myself in a dilemma, seeing that there is no possible way to honor the obligations I have taken on. But there I am—the harm is done. I am now obliged to extricate myself in the least damaging possible way. To one party I owe service, to the other explanations, apologies, amends. But even so—even if I do "all that I possibly can to put things right"—matters will never be *altogether* right. In the circumstances, I am and remain culpable for having made those incompatible promises. A residue of blame continues in place.

But in other circumstances the case will be different. Suppose I promise Smith two hours of help on Saturday and Jones also. But it now unexpectedly eventuates that I am to be frozen into immobility by an evil wizard for all but three hours of the day. Again my obligation will metamorphose into one of giving partial help, due explanations and apologies, and assurances of future aid. But of course the intrusion of unforeseeable circumstances beyond my control removes all moral culpability from the default, and transforms those obligations into changed versions that leave behind no residue of moral culpability. In any case, however, keeping one's obligations compatible insofar as one can manage to do through one's own explicit effort is an important meta-obligation.

Considerations of this sort indicate the existence of higher-level general principles of obligation management, such as the following:

- Honor your obligations.

- Do not shirk your obligations by deliberately putting yourself into circumstances where it will prove impossible for you to meet them.

- Keep your obligations fulfillable: don't get yourself overcommitted.

- Avoid getting yourself entangled in conflicts of obligation.

- Do not go overboard on keeping out of obligation's way. Do not isolate yourself from others just to avoid getting involved with obligations towards them.

- In figuring out what your obligations are do not ignore morally relevant considerations.

— Act on your moral principles: do not simply ignore them when deliberating about your choices.

— Guide your own actions by the same rules of conduct that you are prepared to stipulate for others.

Such rules indicate the existence of meta-obligations: higher-level (second-order) obligations that govern one's appropriate comportment in the management of lower-level (first-order) obligations. What is at issue here are procedural, second-order principles with respect to how we are to conduct our first-order, substantive proceedings. Nevertheless they too count as moral principles and a deliberate violation of them would be blameworthy from the moral point of view.

Consider, for example, the person who deliberately contrives to live a life of Robinson Crusoe-like isolation. While seldom defaulting concrete obligations towards others through contriving to have so few of them, this person is no moral paragon at all. For such an individual nevertheless defaults on that important higher-level obligation towards participation with one's fellows in forging the multilaterally beneficial communal existence that carries in its wake both opportunities and dangers for the moral life.

Deontic metamorphosis is in this way a process shaped pervasively by the operation of higher-level moral principles. Its guiding idea is that of damage-control: "Whenever you cannot for whatever reason honor one of your obligations in its direct and straightforward form, then proceed in a way that minimizes the morally negative consequences that follow from this state of affairs." And as this principle indicates, we cannot always escape—even in the face of unavoidable infeasibilities—from the complex challenges of the moral sphere short of violating the demands of morality itself.

"But when things go unavoidably awry, just how is one to minimize the harm?" That is a very long story. There are, alas, no straightforward rules of resolution. Would that there were! For then the moral life would be made far simpler, much more automatic than it actually is—or realistically can be. The adequate management of our first-order obligations encounters the reefs and shoals of an often difficult and uncooperative world where matters often just do not run in their ordinary course. In the real world, there is no escaping the problems—and opportunities—that the challenges of the moral life hold in store for us.

Chapter Five

MORALITY AND THE
MILITARY PROFESSION

1. INTRODUCTION

THE theme of these deliberations will be the complexity of
military obligation. It must be said straightway, however,
that this matter of obligation of members of the profession of
arms is something that differs only in degree, and not in kind,
from the complexity of human obligation in general. After all,
any adult human being bears a substantial diversity of obligations—to one's employer, to one's client, to one's family, to one's
friend, and so on. All of us owe debts of duty to various individuals and groups—obligations that root in the nature of the different relationships that exist among people. They result from the
sort of role that each one of us plays in the lives and affairs of
others—be it as their employee, their attorney, their brother,
their friend, their neighbor, and so on. In joining the profession
of arms one takes on further special obligations—though, of
course, one does thereby not exit from the events of obligations
in which all people are caught up in.

The obligations that people have are highly differential in
nature. Some are legal, some moral, some merely social and
rooted in the custom of the country. But each such sort of obligation has a certain force and legitimate of its own. And all are
important to maintaining a healthy and fully developed human
existence. No one of them predominates to the exclusion of all
the rest. For example, someone who says to all others "I shall only
give you what is legally your due, nothing else matters to me" and
proceeds to treat all people on this basis—parent, child, friend,
and colleague alike—is literally inhuman. In theory, this sort of
thing is possible. One could write a story about such an individual. But the picture one would draw in the course of this story
would be that of a monster, not of a normal human being.

Some obligations are assumed voluntarily, others are involuntary, and still others are mixed. Your obligations to your par-

ents are involuntary; those to your spouse or employer are assumed voluntary; those to your co-workers or your fellow citizens are mixed—because while you certainly do not choose them, you could, in principle, arrange to have others. Nevertheless, be they voluntary or not, all those various obligations are perfectly real and genuine. The obligations that one *finds* in place are just as authentic as those that one *puts* in place. And one certainly does not eliminate obligations by thinking them inconvenient and wishing they were not there.

Even voluntarily assumed obligations can have involuntary consequences. If unhappy circumstances lead the vessel to shipwreck on a remote island, it may burden the captain with responsibilities for the safety of others that nobody bargained for at the outset, and which neither the captain nor the crew imagined in advance.

Moreover, in taking on new roles and entering into new obligations you do not in general shed the old ones. When you change employers you do, to be sure, exchange your erstwhile employment-related obligations for others, but you do not thereby cancel your obligations to a spouse or to your children. When you become a parent, you do not lose your obligations to your siblings or your fellow citizens. Our duties in life do not cancel one another; they generally become combined and superimposed upon each other.

The coexistence of obligations means that they can compete and conflict. You cannot devote to your children the time you spend with a sick neighbor in the hospital. You cannot appropriately dedicate to your friends and relations the efforts and energies you owe to your employer. It is a fact of life that the obligations that we have will often compete and must, in such situations, be balanced off against each other.

In this life we are all servants of many masters. We have obligations to ourselves and to the other people who play a role in our lives. And it is not always easy to harmonize them—to figure out, say, what is, in the circumstances, due to Caesar and what is due to God. The complexity of obligation is a phenomenon that pervades human life. It is something that every responsible adult has to learn to deal with.

But while this is a general phenomenon, it is one that is particularly acute for members of the military profession. And the reason for this is simple and straightforward. It lies in the fact that the obligation of the military person is—like that of a spouse or a parent—particularly large and pervasive in its scope. In the military, one's duty to one's country, to one's service, and one's unit looms very large indeed. It does not end with the time of day, the location of one's placement, or the extent of one's resources. When the going gets too tough, the discontented spouse can get a divorce, the dissatisfied employee can quit the job, but the reluctant soldier, sailor, or aviator has no easy recourse.

All the same, the obligation of the military person, wide and deep though it is, does not become all-absorbing. It does not automatically overpower and abrogate all other obligations. Many of them remain in place—crowded into a narrower space, perhaps, but still very much present. Nevertheless, for better or for worse, there is something particularly weighty and burdensome about the military person's obligations.

2. Foci of Obligation

Membership in the profession of arms involves many foci of obligation. Five of them are paramount importance:

—the chain of command

—the service

—the nation

—civilization

—humanity at large

Every one of these has its own characteristics and its own ramifications. Let me say a brief word about each.

The Chain of Command. For the military person, the first and most obvious source of obligation is clearly those duties that come into being through the injunctions of those whom the military system has emplaced in positions of authority. The duty of obedience to legal command—personal preferences notwithstanding—is the most basic and definitive commitment of those who belong to the profession of arms. Irrespective of whether one's affiliation is voluntarily self-generated (via enlistment) or generated through the action of one's fellow citizens (via a draft), one is by law, custom, and hoary practice bound to this chain of command, and in consequence subject to the separate and stringent code of justice to which the military stands bound.

However, if one's obligation to the chain of command were all—if it cancelled all of one's other obligations—then the life of a member of the military profession would be much simpler than it is. It is precisely because this most characteristic and weighty of soldierly duties is not all that there is to it that the complexity of military obligation arises.

The Service. Beyond the chain of command lies first of all "the service"—the entire organization in its historical unity—to which the chain of command gives a concrete temporary embodiment. When it does its work well and serves its function appropriately, the chain of command generally implements the best interests of the service. But every once in a while things go wrong. And then the conscientious professional has to ask him or herself the difficult question of whether the particular orders at hand or those larger interests are to prevail. The legendary supply sergeant on Wake Island who, adhering to standing regulations, is reported to have made his troops sign receipts for the live ammunition being issued them as the Japanese were storming ashore would be a clear example of someone who didn't get his competing duties properly prioritized.

The Nation, the Civilization, and Humanity at Large. Beyond the service there loom the large issues of one's country, one's civilization, and also humanity at large. In being a member of the profession of arms, one does not cease to be a citizen, a responsible person, or a human being. And at those levels of relationship, issues of potentially conflicting obligations also arise. Even in the heat of war there are some sorts of militarily useful things that are just not done. (One does not, for example, clear minefields by marching enemy civilians across them—or, for that matter, even prisoners of war.)

The military profession is, in the final analysis, in the business of killing people. But even when this is taken as a given, morality and common sense require that there has to be a due proportioning of ends to means. It is senseless to use a bulldozer to squash a fly. And it is wrong to waste human life wholesale where retail killing is enough. The military person is, or should be, a disciplined professional, and not a terrorist who is prepared to kill hundreds to finish off one intended victim.

For the military profession is not *just* a matter of killing people. Even actual warfare has among other dimensions, and the complexity of military obligation is amply manifested in such other contexts.

To illustrate this, let us examine some concrete examples. Specifically, we shall consider four episodes which clearly bring to view the intricacies of military obligation. These episodes have been chosen, quite deliberately, from the pages of German rather than American military experience. For when a situation comes too close to home, our personal loyalties and ideological leanings prevent our being able to view the matter with the objectivity and detachment that is needed in order to see clearly and objectively just what the issues are. Geographic and cultural distance improves the prospects of making a detached and dispassionate appraisal of the fundamental principles at stake.

3. Episode No. 1: The General and the Danish Jews

In the middle of World War II, the German occupation forces in Denmark were commanded by Infantry-General (General der Infanterie) Heinrich von Henneken, a professional soldier of proven ability. His was not, however, an autonomous command, for his military jurisdiction was subordinate on all matters relating to specifically political affairs to the primary of the Ambassador. Since Denmark came under German control by political surrender rather than military conquest, the power of control was vested in the Foreign Office in Berlin, to which, in effect, von Henneken was ultimately answerable.

In September of 1943, orders went forth from Berlin decreeing that a state of emergency should be declared in Denmark and all Jews rounded up for deportation. On 23 September, von Henneken requested a postponement of this operation. Pleading a shortage of manpower support, he simply dug in his heels. When Berlin persisted, he strongly represented the impracticability and the undesirability of any army involvement in the operation, insisting that this would "injure the prestige of the Wehrmacht at home and in foreign countries." Instructions to the contrary notwithstanding, he refused the use of military personnel in the round-up and generally minimized cooperation. His intransigence created a delay during which most Danish Jews were successfully evacuated to Sweden.

The case of von Henneken affords a clear and striking illustration of a soldier who put the best interests and good repute of his service ahead of the demands of the chain of command. As best as one can tell, von Henneken's motivation was—as far as external appearance went, at any rate—not so much a humanitarian compassion for the fate of the victims, as a sense of the inappropriateness of involving the military in their victimization. His concern was for the good name and repute of his service, taking the position that there are certain sorts of things that a self-respecting army just does not do. As far as von Henneken was concerned, the best interests of the service took priority over any mere mechanical obedience to instructions from higher authority. Fortunately for him, despite the irritation of Nazi authorities in Berlin, friends in high places were able to protect von Henneken against unpleasant personal consequences—although this was something of which he had no prior assurance at the time of action.[1]

4. EPISODE NO. 2: THE ARMY AND THE COUNTRY

Let us next turn to another, rather different sort of episode. Some time ago, General Augusto Pinochet, Chile's former long-term head, and then still continuing army commander, set off an international furor by his remarks in an address to the Rotary club in Santiago.[2] Using strong and biting terms, he characterized the postwar transformation of the German military as an unmitigated disaster. According to Pinochet, the democratization of the German army and its acceptance of the individual rights of its members had brought a once proud military organization near to ruin. Pinochet viewed with alarm the prospect that there might be Chilean disciples of the generals who built the new German army in a way that undermined the longstanding Prussian tradition of strict discipline, unquestioning obedience, and absence of discussion. (After all, the Chilean military inclines to view their army as the last Prussian-style army still in existence.) Pinochet accordingly castigated the German commanders "who betrayed that institution by trying to convert it into an army of inferior values." No doubt echoing a body of sentiment in the German military itself, Pinochet took the line that from a strictly service point of view, the "democratization" of the military is a step towards its emasculation. Pinochet characterized the officers responsible for the changes as "the biggest traitors Germany has had with respect to its army."

Pinochet's remarks understandably provoked an immediate reaction from the German government—and from the German military as well. Their spokesmen responded by stressing the idea that "The soldier of today has to be a citizen." And they observed that the change in the German military system since then was intended "to harmonize obedience and military discipline with the principles and values of liberty and human dignity."

As the German military spokesmen emphasized in response to Pinochet's strictures, a duty to the service and its strictly military values has to be balanced and coordinated—in contemporary Western democracies at any rate—with a duty to the nation and to the values that its military is instituted to defend. Against Pinochet's narrow professional traditionalism, the German military spokesmen gave voice to a widespread acknowledgment that the interests and values of the country and its citizenry have to play a significant role in the management of military affairs. As they represented the matter, the modern soldier's duty to the civic values of the community is not less significant than his duty to strictly military values of the service.

5. Episode No. 3: The General and The City: Is Paris Burning?

Sometimes members of the profession of arms come up against obligations of even a more far-reaching and—so to speak—ominous sort. This is exemplified by our next illustrative episode.[3]

In 1944, the German commander of the Paris region was one General Dietrich von Choltitz. He was a Prussian general of the old school. A third-generation professional soldier, he had served in the airborne infantry with impressive success. He had led the unit that made the initial thrust into Holland and had devastated Rotterdam. Much further from home, he had commanded the regiment that took the Russian stronghold of Sebastopol in the Crimea.

As the allies were now converging on Paris, Hitler ordered an all-out, house-to-house defense of the city. The high command, the OKW under von Rundstedt, put demolition teams at von Choltitz' disposal and ordered him to mount a Stalingrad-like defense of the city.

As the man on the spot, von Choltitz saw the matter in a different light. He realized that an all-out defense of Paris would lead to an immense loss of life, since there was no prospect of evacuating the civilian population. He also believed that an effective effort to hold the city was ultimately impracticable, and that a house-to-house defense could achieve no significant goal beyond a modest delay of the Allies' overall advance, and that any serious steps in this direction would result in the physical destruction of Europe's most beautiful city. His considered professional judgment was that no valid military purpose could be served by an all-out effort to defend Paris. But orders are orders. Von Choltitz was in a deep and painful dilemma. And he resolved it in a bold and radical way.

Von Choltitz simply cut the chain of command. He ignored his orders, contacted the Allies, and arranged to surrender the city with minimal resistance. There is little doubt that von Choltitz' actions verged on the outright treasonable. And yet it could be argued that he was, in a way, justified—that his obligation to the chain of command was outweighed by obligations and interests of a higher order. Von Choltitz had made a very hard and very dangerous decision. As he was led away to internment by his Allied captors, unknowing Frenchmen spat at him in the street. They would have done better to build him a statue.[4]

Von Choltitz realized that nations and peoples survive wars. Win or lose, Germans and French are destined to share the land-mass of Europe as neighbors. And he recognized that an utterly pointless destruction of people and cultural treasures would poison the atmosphere and render peaceful coexistence difficult if not impossible for many years to come. From one point of view—that of the chain of command—we could say that von Choltitz failed in his duty: perhaps even that he was a traitor. And yet it is difficult to deny that a responsible member of the profession of arms has obligations that extend beyond the chain of command, obligations to support the best interests of his country—and sometimes even the higher interests encompassed in the values that the traditions of the country profess.

6. Episode No. 4: The Anti-Hitler Conspiracy

And this brings us to the fourth and last episode. It is undoubtedly the most drastic one—the 1944 attempt to assassinate Hitler.

There is no need here to describe the details—the story of Colonel Count Stauffenberg and his associates is too well known. The bomb that blew up on the wrong side of the conference table's supporting pedestal, the rallying of the shaken Führer's authority, the collapse of the conspiracy in the face of the opposition of military loyalists, the swift and cruel end of the conspirators and their sympathizers—all these are circumstances that do not need elaboration here. Rather what matters for present purposes is that this was not a matter of the rising of an outraged populace or of a counterstroke launched by disaffected opposition politicians, but a conspiracy launched from deep within the traditional beliefs and values of the German military establishment.

The conspirators worked under difficult conditions. In some ways, they were less than highly competent, in others, they were just plain unlucky. But the important consideration, for my present purposes, is that these officers were actuated not by considerations of personal gain or political advantage, but acted out of a genuine—and surely not altogether misguided—sense of duty to the German army, the German nation, and the German people. While these officers indeed violated their pledge of loyalty to Reich and Führer, they nevertheless acted out a deep sense of obligation to their service, their country, their national traditions, and their higher duties.[5]

7. SOME *LESSONS*

The four episodes we have just considered illustrate the complexity and potential conflicts of the obligations of those who exercise military authority. In von Hennecken's case, he had to choose between his good name as a soldier and the honor of his service on the one hand, and obedience to lawful orders on the other. Again, those German officers who responded to Pinochet placed the health of their service and the political values of their country ahead of the traditional values and interests of its military establishment. Von Choltitz in Paris found the awesome choice between his straightforward duties as an officer on the one side and a commitment to the long-range best interests of his country and his dedication to civilized values on the other. Finally, von Stauffenberg and his co-conspirators put their lives on the line in placing their soldier's honor ahead of their soldier's oath, and setting what they saw as the best interests of their service and of their country ahead of unquestioning obedience to constituted authority.

All of these cases exemplify in a particularly dramatic way the agonizing situations arising when an officer faces a complex choice among conflicting obligations in situations fraught with difficulty and danger.

No doubt the particular episodes we have considered involve rather extreme situations of conflicts of duty. But precisely because of the extremity of such cases, they serve to highlight sharply the complexity of obligation and the potential conflict of duty that—in some less dramatic way—faces virtually every responsible member of the profession of arms.

Most American officers of today will almost certainly be fortunate in never having to face such conflict situations at a high level of visibility and historical significance, in circumstances where the pull of conflicting duty to chain of command, to country, to civilization—and indeed even to oneself as an individual human being—come into conflict with one another. But every military officer faces less dramatic cases of this general sort of situation some of the time. This simply goes with the territory of being responsible for matters concerned with the well-being and even the lives of other people.

The fact is, that at one point or another, every officer faces difficult choices among competing obligations. For the exercise of command responsibilities over the actions and situations of other people can all too easily create a condition of conflicting obligations—though (mercifully) usually of a minor and undramatic kind. But even in their milder forms, such experiences will bring home a realization that the complexity of military obligation is not an abstract theoretical exercise, but something real that grabs you in the heart, the chest, and the stomach.

All the same, the underlying principle is a straightforward one. America's splendid Declaration of Independence has it that all people have certain inalienable rights. But rights, of course, are correlative with duties—and people accordingly have inalienable duties as well—obligations that we can resign no more than one can resign one's status as a human being. And these inalienable duties to ourselves and to our fellow humans are by their very nature such that one does not lay them aside when one puts on the military uniform of one's country. Do what we will, we cannot escape those duties—nor yet what comes with them: the judgment of one's fellows, one's friends, one's family, and—least of all—oneself.

All of these different foci of obligation—one's lawful orders, one's service, one's country, one's values—represent valid and appropriate commitments upon every officer—commitments that make very real and pressing claims, be they legal or moral. When these claims clash with one another, there just are no easy solutions and no mechanical formulas for working out the answer. Like any mature individual in a responsible position in life, an officer needs the ability to resolve conflicts thoughtfully—to examine an issue on every relevant side and to give each element of a difficult and controversial situation its due.

The conflicting claims that arise from complex obligations must be confronted and weighed and balanced and resolved. All one can do is to work things out in one's heart and mind as thoughtfully and conscientiously as one can—and then do what one has to do. There are no simple, automatic rules, and to respond in a simpleminded and automatic way to problems of the sort at issue is to court disaster. One has no alternative but to worry and fret and sweat.

But one point decries particular emphasis. It is this: When one experiences the responsibilities incumbent upon a military officer, one does not cease to be a citizen and one does not cease to be a human being.

This may perhaps sound rather simplistic and naive. But it has substantial consequences. For it means that the officer, though indeed just another link in the chain of command, is nevertheless not a mere automaton responding to the will of others, but continues bearing responsibility for oneself as a person. "Following orders" is a crucial part of the soldier's code, but it is not the only one.

The officer cannot look simply to the wishes of a superior, or simply to the practice of the group, to what "the others" are doing, but continues as an individual, as a citizen and as a human being—as someone who must to his or her own self be true, as someone who must act as a person in the light of his or her own values.

A fundamental recognition of right and wrong—a conscience, in short—is what makes one into a responsible person. It is a resource that every officer does and should have. It is what marks one as a responsible individual agent, capable of being answerable for his or her acts, even in the fact of contrary custom and group disapproval. It is a manifestation of that most admirable and awesome human quality—the willingness to assume responsibility and stand by one's obligations as one sees them even where risks for oneself are involved.

The fact is that in the larger scheme of things, the quality of *moral* courage is no less desirable and no less admirable in a military officer than the quality of *physical* courage.[6]

Notes

1. For a fuller account of this episode see Raul Helberg, *The Destruction of the European Jews*, Vol. 2 (New York, 1985), pp. 558-68.

2. For a detailed report on this episode see the 8 September 1990 dispatch from Santiago filed by Shirley Christian of the *New York Times*, and published in that newspaper on 9 September 1990 under the title "Pinochet Irks the West Germans With a Potshot at Their Military."

3. The episode is described in detail in Larry Collins and Dominique Lapreire, *Is Paris Burning?* (New York: Simon & Schuster, 1965).

4. Von Choltitz survived to write his memoirs, *Soldat unter Soldaten*, published in 1951.

5. A useful source of information and appraisal is Hans-Adolf Jacobsen (ed.), *July 20, 1944: The German Opposition to Hitler as Viewed by Foreign Historians* (Bonn: Press and Information Office of the Federal Government, 1989).

6. This essay is a revised version of an address on "The Complexity of Military Obligation," presented to the junior class of the Air Force Academy in Colorado Springs on 15 November 1990. The address was published by the Air Force Academy as the third Joseph A. Reich Sr. Distinguished Lecture on War, Morality, and the Military Profession.

Chapter Six

MORAL OBLIGATION
AND THE REFUGEE

THE issue to be addressed here is a straightforward-looking question of applied moral philosophy: Do refugees owe any special debt of moral obligation to the nation and society that provides them with their refuge? To all appearances, this not uninteresting question is one that has been neglected by popular moralists or moral philosophers alike.[1]

It must be stressed from the start that this discussion will concern itself with duties and obligations that relate to the *moral* rather than *legal* aspects of the issue—not with what the law requires, but with those duties and obligations that inhere in a conscientious concern for what people owe to one another within the context of a rightly ordered life.

Note, to begin with, political or religious refugees are a very special sort of immigrant. They are not escapists seeking to be rid of a pressing creditor or a difficult spouse. They are not comfort-seekers looking for a kinder climate or more congenial surroundings. Nor are they opportunists searching for a better economic environment for employment or investment—or for bright opportunities for an appealing career or a satisfying life-style. Actual refugees come to their country of refuge not so much because they want to, as because they must. For them, the new homeland is, in the first instance, not an opportunity but a necessity, because it offers a refuge against the storm of oppression, discrimination, or persecution.

Now what about obligations? When refugees arrive in their new homeland, they enter upon a stage whose action is already well under way, a going concern of facilities and institutions to whose creation—all too obviously—they themselves have made no contribution. Their new country provides them with a ready-made environment for living at no further cost or sacrifice to themselves. This, clearly, is a benefit for which the new refugee-resident is indebted to others—and he certainly has no moral right or entitlement to expect it as a free gift.

Or is this indeed so? It could be said, after all, that this happens to all of us at birth. All of us are, in a way, refugees in this life, emigrating from the state of nonbeing into this ready-made world to whose creation we have nowise contributed.

But there is scope for counter-argumentation here, based in the idea of inheritance. In one's native land, one's forefathers have in the past contributed their efforts and energies to making the society a "going concern." Whatever property they accumulated privately they disposed of in their wills as best the laws of the land would let them. And the public fruits of their efforts and energies—their general contribution to the society and its resources—become part of the social legacy of the community at large to be inherited by their fellow countrymen. It would clearly be inappropriate to deny the claims of inheritance of those whose families have struggled for generations to bring into being an economy, a society, and a culture of whose resources refugees are beneficiaries as of the day they step across the borders of the land. The "native" can accordingly claim a share of the public goods by right of inheritance. The immigrant can make no such claim. So it is not implausible to argue that the refugee owes a significant debt—not merely of gratitude but also of justice—to the nation and society that provides him refuge.

Refugees have in general found the prior setting of their lives made intolerable for political or social reasons. Casting about for a more viable alternative, they have at last succeeded in finding a new "homeland." For such refugees, the immediate object of concern is survival, given the urgent dangers of the moment. It is, no doubt, only with the passage of years that refugees come to realize in distant retrospect what the citizenry of that new homeland are entitled to ask of them—what sorts of expectations they are warranted in entertaining and how the entire transaction looks from *their* point of view. But sooner or later the conscientious refugee will come around to this recognition. For even the most rudimentary attention to the facts cannot but bring home to refugees that their welfare and well-being—their livelihood and perhaps their very life—is due to the willingness of the host country to take them into its midst. The host society extended its hospitality in the hour of need.[2] Owing nothing, it gave much—not only safety, but opportunity as well.

What can be said of the special obligation that results? What can the host society rightfully expect of the refugee?

The debt which a refugee owes to his new homeland can be characterized straightforwardly. For it is simply the general obligation of good citizenship—albeit in a particularly substantial degree.

This simple single idea of course ramifies out into a score of special obligations: putting one's hand to the work of communal production, obeying the laws of the land, shouldering the burdens of good citizenship (military service, jury duty, voting, and the like). The least that the conscientious refugee can do for the society that affords him refuge is to assume cheerfully the obligations of conscientious communal membership. And in particular, the conscientious refugee also owes it to his new homeland to support the values and traditions that characterize its social order. It is, after all, these values and traditions that have shaped the society which sheltered and nourished the refugee in the hour of need. And a combination of gratitude and obligation thus binds him in an implicit social contract of sorts not only to the laws but also to this underlying "spirit of the laws" of the host society.[3] And so, the morally conscientious refugee must in due season shoulder the burden of a social conscientiousness that makes him, insofar as possible, an asset to the community rather than a liability.

Does the refugee owe his new homeland an unquestioning approbation of its programs and policies? Surely not. It is clear that no moral impediment need prevent the refugee from criticizing the host society where it fails to live up to its own appropriate values and ideals. Quite to the contrary, this generic duty of good citizenship should for him be something of a special obligation. But it should never be allowed to serve as an excuse for a failure of loyalty and attachment to the newfound homeland.

These considerations lead to the question: What is the *ground* (basis, rationale) of the obligations of a refugee towards the nation and society that provided him or her with a refuge (asylum) in time of need?

The basic fact is that refugees are immigrants of a very special sort—ones who, by the very nature of their situation, have incurred particularly pressing responsibilities and obligations. These obligations ultimately root in a social contract of sorts, an implicit argument between the refugee and the nation and society that gives him the refuge. A personalized compact is in operation through a tacit and, as it were, hypothetical bargain:

"You take me in; I will bend my efforts to ensure that you will be the better off for my presence."

The analogy of the guest is relevant here—someone who is invited into someone's home and treated as part of the family. To fail to be helpful and cooperative, good natured and patient, etc., is to run afoul not only of the requirements of good manners, but those of morality as well. Failure in gratitude is a defect that is particularly unseemly in the case of a refugee. In his case one can say that patriotism in the highest and most positive sense of the term—as concerns dedication to the country's best interests—is something mandatory.

There arises, to be sure, the interesting question of the refugee who arrives in a country that goes bad—the white Russian refugee, say, who arrives in Germany in time to be caught up in the Nazi debacle. Are we to see him as obliged to become more Nazi than the Fuhrer himself on the preceding principles of gratitude and tacit agreement? Surely not! For it is clear that the moral weight of such obligations can never override the larger duties of humanity and humaneness that lie at the very core of the moral duties that people owe to one another. The obligations at issue are geared to the host country's best interests, not to its aggrandisement.

A small-scale tempest of discussions has recently brewed up about whether "political obligations" arise from considerations of gratitude.[4] Several points deserve to be stressed in this connection:

First off, the very idea of a "political obligation" has its problems. We all realize what *legal* obligations and what *moral/ ethical* obligations are, but the idea of "*political* obligations" confronts us with a puzzle. The only reasonably straightforward way to solve this puzzle is to construe *political* obligation as encompassing the sum-total of our legal and moral obligations to act in a certain way in matters connected with politics. We would, accordingly, class as "political obligations" both the (legal) obligation of public officials to provide an accounting for the disbursement of public funds placed at their disposal, and the (moral) obligation of elected representatives to respond truthfully to a constituent's question as to whether or not they have decided to vote for some item of pending legislation.

Given such an understanding of "political obligation," it becomes clear that in many or most cases political obligations cannot appropriately be derived from considerations of gratitude. For example, one is not obliged—either legally or morally—to support, in circumstances where a better-qualified rival is on the scene, a congressman who shared his cab from the airport to town. On the other hand, there will—clearly—be *some* instances where gratitude can engender a "political obligation" in the specified sense. For example, if you and I represent neighboring districts, and I found it helpful to enlist your support in campaigning on my behalf during a difficult election year, it would clearly be morally questionable—in the absence of strong and cogent countervailing reasons—for you to deny me similar aid on another occasion. In such circumstances you are, clearly, placed under a "political obligation" (in the moral mode) by considerations of gratitude.

It seems clear from this standpoint that while various sorts of "political obligation" cannot appropriately be grounded in considerations of gratitude, there will indeed be others that can be so grounded. And, in particular, it would clearly be a morally indefensible act of ingratitude regarding benefits extended for the refugee to set at naught those (political) burdens which are part and parcel of good citizenship in the country which provides him the benefit of a refuge.[5]

What is at issue here is thus not only a matter of gratitude, but also one of justice. That the refugees' presence in their midst should prove needlessly burdensome for those who sheltered them in the hour of need is clearly unjustifiable. Until they took those refugees unto themselves, the citizenry of the new homeland owed them nothing; the obligations of those citizens —such as they are—were to their predecessors, their neighbors, their fellow countrymen. The refugee was an extraneous element in the equation. That refugees should place avoidable burdens upon those who have, alike in generic intent and specific effect, been their benefactors would clearly be unconscionable from the moral point of view.

It is illuminating in this regard to ask the question: Just what goes amiss in the moral order when the moral obligations of gratitude that are incurred by refugees are *not* honored? For, clearly, several crucial things do indeed go seriously amiss:

1. A violence to virtues: lack of gratitude, of due appreciation for benefits extended.

2. A failure in duties: the violation of tacit agreement, the breech of a social contract—of the tacit bargain struck when the refugee was accepted into the new homeland ("You take me in; I'll foster your interests and support your cause").

3. A fostering of ill consequences: in particular, a poisoning of the well for others (How can the nation/society as readily accommodate new refugees when the earlier ones have shown themselves to be facilitators of evil rather than good as perpetrators of a kind of social vandalism that diminishes the quality of life for people?).

The refugee who willfully fails to honor such moral obligations is thereby morally reprehensible in ways that may differ in degree but not in kind from the condition of those involved in other sorts of moral transgression.

A further issue fraught with moral overtones is the question of the refugee's relationship to the former homeland. At first, of course, one can expect little but distaste and dismay. One does not lightly tear up one's roots and abandon the comfortable familiarities of the land of one's fathers; terrible things must have happened to drive one away. But gradually time works its inevitable changes. A new generation comes to the fore that had no part in the wrongs of the past. New conditions come about; persons and attitudes, practices and policies change. In due course (if all goes well) the land of a later generation is a very different land. And then it clearly becomes inappropriate to visit the sins of the fathers upon the children. (In point of inheritance the situation of goods and evils is asymmetric from the moral point of view; gratitude and recrimination stand on a different footing.)

In these circumstances, it would clearly be improper for the refugee to let the increasingly irrelevant wrongs of a bygone time intrude upon the changing scenes of a living present. And irrespective of any present feelings, it would be morally improper for the refugee to foster hostility between the new homeland and the abandoned one, letting the bitter experiences of one's own personal past be the occasion for impeding the important and salutary work of a reconciliation among peoples and nations. Among the many obligations that a refuge owes his new homeland is surely this—to avoid making its relations with other countries and peoples less benign and less mutually beneficial than make good sense in the prevailing circumstances. Working actively for a reconciliation is perhaps more than can be asked of him, but he should surely not impede it. Hatred is generally a bad counsellor in human affairs—to say nothing of its negativity from the moral point of view that is at issue here.

A particularly complex issue is posed by the question of the refugee's stand with respect to other, later refugees. Just what are his moral obligations in this regard?

The issue involves a delicate balance. Having himself found refuge, it would clearly be quite inappropriate for a refugee to take the negative line on others, encouraging a policy of pulling up the drawbridge and slamming the gates on those who find themselves in a position similar to that which the refugee himself occupied a brief time ago. To some extent, it is clearly the refugee's duty to help to assure that the opportunities which proved so critical for himself are also available to others. On the other hand, it would also be unjustifiable to have a country go overboard with the admission of refugees—to admit more of them than it can absorb without injury to its quality of life and the viability of its cultural, social, and political traditions. In this regard, then, the stance of the conscientious refugee must be one of a sensible balance between undesirable extremes.

In summary, the moral dimension of refugeeship requires that the attitudes and actions of the conscientious refugee should be conditioned by three fundamental principles:

(i) a gratitude that is properly due to those who have extended a helping hand to oneself in one's hour of need—a gratitude that calls for some effort to make the advancement of their interests part of one's own.

(ii) a due sense of the obligations implicit in the social contract between the refugee and citizenry of the sheltering country that he will not only try to avoid being a burden but will bend his efforts to ensure that the country of refuge would be the better off for his presence.

(iii) a sympathetic and sensitive concern for the condition of others who find themselves in similar distressing circumstances, and now also require the safety of a refuge.

The fundamental moral factors that are at work here—gratitude, good citizenship, fellow-feeling—are universal virtues. But the particular circumstances of the refugee mean that they exert their bearing upon him in a special and characteristically emphatic way.

Given the nature of the situation, the refugee is someone to whom the sheltering country has extended benefits "above and beyond the call of ordinary duty." And it is clear that, from the moral point of view at any rate, an acceptance of these special benefits also demands the acceptance of certain special responsibilities, and requires of its beneficiaries an exertion towards productive contributions that go above and beyond the ordinary call. The law, of course, makes no distinction between the duties and obligations of native-born citizens and those who came as refugees. In this regard, then, as in various others, the demands of morality will exceed those basic demands that the law makes on everyone alike. It would, of course, be very questionable to contemplate transmuting those moral obligations into legal ones. But this does not render them any less cogent. (It is one of the regrettable features of the present ethos that many people think—very wrongly indeed—that those obligations that are not subject to the sanctions of the law are for this reason somehow rendered null and void.)[6]

Notes

1. It is, however, of particular interest to me because my family left Nazi Germany as refugees in 1938, when I myself was nine years of age.

2. The case of *illegal* refugees is, to be sure, a rather different one. Here, that "taking in" and "hospitality" are, at best, euphemisms. But in this, circumstance increases rather than diminishes those *moral* burdens.

3. The obligations at issue also impact in a somewhat diminished way upon that special subcategory of refugees, the exiles, whose refugeedom is only temporary—who are, as it were, transit passengers awaiting the possibility of return to a place they continue to regard as home. In point of the demands and obligations incumbent upon refugees at large, their condition differs only in degree and not in kind from that of those not leaving their native land on a more permanent basis.

4. The discussion goes back to Plato's *Crito*, and has more recently been resumed in J. P. Plamenatz, *Consent Freedom and Political Obligation* (Oxford, 1968; 2nd. ed.). Recent concern was stimulated by A. John Simmons, *Moral Principles and Political Obligations* (Princeton, 1979), see esp. Chap. 7, "Gratitude." See also Claudia Card, "Gratitude and Obligation," *American Philosophical Quarterly* (1988), pp. 118-27; A. D. M. Walker, "Political Obligation and the Argument for Gratitude," *Philosophy and Public Affairs*, vol. 17 (1988), pp. 191-211; as well as George Klosko's papers: "Political Obligation and Gratitude," *Philosophy and Public Affairs*, vol. 18 (1989), pp. 353-58, and "Four Arguments Against Political Obligation from Gratitude," *Public Affairs Quarterly*, vol. 5 (1991), pp. 33-48. There is also a response to the former Klosko paper by A. D. M. Walker, "Obligations of Gratitude and Political Obligation," *Philosophy and Public Affairs*, vol. 18 (1989), pp. 359-72.

5. In his book mentioned above, A. J. Simmons dismisses the idea of

political obligations on grounds that ultimately root in "doubts about benefits provided by groups of persons" because "where a group of persons is concerned, there is very seldom anything like a reason, common to them all, for which the benefit was provided" (pp. 187-88), considerations which lead Simmons to reject the idea of debts of gratitude to institutions. What is mysterious here is (i) why a uniformity of reason should be crucial, and (ii) why a benefit extended by social (rather than individual) decision should not engender correspondingly socially oriented indebtedness. Admittedly, the extent to which one should be grateful to a benefactor depends to some extent on the intention of the benefactor in performing the action that provides the benefit at issue. But there can be little doubt that a nation that adopts and implements an immigration policy which provides asylum and refuge to the citizens of other countries in situations of necessity thereby deserves credit for good intentions.

6. This essay was written for a Festschrift for my colleague and fellow refugee Adolf Grünbaum: John Earman *et al.* (eds.), *Philosophical Problems of the Internal and External World* (Pittsburgh and Konstanz: University of Pittsburgh Press/Universitätsverlag Konstanz, 1994).

Chapter Seven

CONCRETIZATION QUANDARIES AND PRAGMATIC ANOMALIES

1. CONCRETIZATION QUANDARIES: A PRACTICAL PERSPECTIVE

A concretization quandary arises when it is a good idea to do A, but the only way to do so concretely is by doing A_1 or A_2 or A_3 (etc.), while nevertheless doing each of these A_i is a bad idea. In such situations there is no concrete way of realizing a generically desirable objective.

Thus recall the story of the princess whose father is a kingly ogre who will release her from his paternal thralldom only on condition of marrying the princeling of some neighboring kingdom. But all of the available princelings are quite ineligible: one is too ugly, another too stupid, a third too loutish, and the like. For the princess, marriage is seemingly a good idea. Yet each of the feasible alternatives for realizing this objective is unsuitable and unacceptable.

Or consider the plight of the younger son of an impoverished aristocrat. He finds himself so situated that "taking up an appropriate career" is somewhere between eminently desirable and absolutely necessary. But each of the acceptable alternatives is infeasible; he is too cowardly for the army, too hydrophobic for the navy, too sceptical for the church, and so on.

Or again: the president of the country is a catastrophe, and it is clear to all Ruritanians that there needs to be a change. Nobody questions the abstract desirability of "electing a new president." But unhappily each of the candidates who has made their way onto the ballot has some fatal flaw. For each *particular* prospect, "X ought to be president in place of the incumbent" can be rejected out of hand.

A quandary of concretization arises when a certain generic act is abstractly desirable but yet this can be accomplished only in various particular ways each of which is concretely undesirable. The person facing such a situation looks to the pursuit of an evident desideratum, but is emplaced in the uncomfortable and unhappy position that there is no acceptable way to get there from here.

A schematic illustration of this phenomenon is readily produced. We have a choice between performing A and not-A in circumstances where A can (only) be realized in one or another of three versions (A_1, A_2, A_3). And the situation we now confront stands as follows: A is realizable only via the several concrete A_i—so that $A \leftrightarrow (\exists i) A_i$—but while realizing A is desirable, and with it $(\exists i) A_i$, it nevertheless remains false that for any individual i, des A_i obtains. Such circumstances accordingly combine two considerations:

1. That A be done (or realized) *somehow* is—in the abstract—something desirable: des $(\exists i) A_i$.

but nevertheless

2. There is no *particular* version A_i of A such that it is desirable to do (or realize) A_i: $-(\exists i)$ des A_i.

Accordingly, what the existence of concretization quandaries demonstrates and illustrates is that we do *not* in general have at our disposal the implication:

(T1)   des $(\exists i) A_i \rightarrow (\exists i)$ des A_i.

From a logician's standpoint, the perplex at issue roots in the fact that the existential quantifier and the des-operator do not commute. But of course what is at issue is not a mere bit of logical legerdermain but an actual existential perplexity.

The basic difficulty is that abstract desiderata have to be realized in concrete circumstances. And in such concrete circumstances we never have that abstract desideratum in and by itself; rather its concretization is invariably accompanied by a penumbra of circumstantial detail—we never have *just A* but always *A-with-Z* for some circumstantial addendum. And the prospect arises that each and every available circumstantial addendum offsets and negates the positivity at issue with A. The performance of what is, in and of itself, a perfectly proper act in A may—in the existing circumstances—saddle us with collateral negativities, with the result that there just is no acceptable concretization of an abstractly appropriate desideratum.

A larger lesson emerges. Life proceeds in an imperfect world where certain abstractly desirable acts cannot be concretely realized because each and every one of the available specific and concrete ways in which this realization can actually be achieved involves collaterally incidental deficits that negate—in those particular circumstances—the general benefit at issue. From the practical point of view, the world's arrangements may prove to be far from ideal.

2. A More General Approach

Does the converse of (T1) hold? That is, do we have:

(T2) $(\exists i)$ des $A_i \rightarrow$ des $(\exists i) A_i$

Does being *conditionally* desirable (i.e., desirable in *some* circumstance) entail being *abstractly* desirable (desirable in itself)? Clearly not. Consider the situation of the distasteful antidote. Taking the substance is conditionally desirable (once the poison has been ingested) but clearly is not abstractly desirable in and of itself.

From the angle of this general perspective there arises a whole host of questions about implication relationships that deserve to be surveyed systematically. Four theses are now at issue:

a: $(\forall i)$ des A_i, "A is *distributively* desirable—desirable unconditionally in any and every case"

b: des $(\forall i) A_i$, "A is *universally* desirable—desirable absolutely and unqualifiedly"

c: $(\exists i)$ des A_i, "A is *conditionally* desirable—desirable in some cases or under some conditions"

d: des $(\exists i) A_i$, "A is *abstractly* or *generically* desirable—desirable indefinitely or in the abstract"

The possible implication relationships that obtain among these propositions can be inventoried as follows:

$\rightarrow$	a	b	c	d
a	+	(1)	(2)	(3)
b	(4)	+	(5)	(6)
c	(7)	(8)	+	(9)
d	(10)	(11)	(12)	+

The redundant implications along the diagonal obviously obtain (as indicated by +). Let us consider the status of the others:

(1)   + This presumably holds seeing that (1) is equivalent to the eminently plausible: non-des $(\forall i)\, A \rightarrow (\exists i)$ non-des A_i.)

(2)   + By mere logic.

(3)   + Since (1) → (3).

(4)   + This presumably holds seeing that des $(\forall i)\, A_i$ and $(\exists i)$ non-des A_i are to all appearances incompatible.

(5)   + Since (4) → (5).

(6)   + By mere logic.

(7)   − By mere logic.

(8)   − By our rejection of T2, since (8) → (9).

(9) = T2   − By our rejection of T2. [Recall the distasteful antidote.]

(10)   − By our rejection of T1, since (10) → (12).

(11)   − By mere logic.

(12) = T1   − By our rejection of T1. [The concretization quandary situation.]

Prescinding from the diagonal, it can be said that the top half of the implication table is uniformly + and the bottom half uniformly −.

Note that the following implication relationships obtain:

(7) + (1) → (8)

(7) + (3) → (9)

(8) + (4) → (7)

(8) + (6) → (9)

(9) + (10) → (7)

(9) + (11) → (8)

Moreover, note that given (1) – (9), any one of (10) – (12) yields the other two, since:

(10) + (1) → (11)

(10) + (2) → (12)

(11) + (4) → (10)

(11) + (5) → (12)

(12) + (7) → (10)

(12) + (8) → (11)

Given (1) – (6), it thus follows that in order to avoid $(T_1) = (12)$ and $(T_2) = (9)$ we must reject *all* of the series (7) – (12). Negativity must prevail throughout the bottom half of the implication table, except for the diagonal.

But this is not the end of the story.

3. A Kantian Demarche: A Moral Perspective

The situation becomes altered when we turn from *practical* desirability to *moral* desirability—desirability from a specifically and unalloyedly moral point of view. For here we (or at any rate some of us) will sympathize with Kant's well-known insistence that *moral* desirability (moral appropriateness) is something special through having a feature that differentiates it crucially from desirability in general, namely the feature of universalizability.

Accordingly, let us consider the universalization principle that lies at the heart of Kant's moral theory:

m-des $A_n \rightarrow (\forall i)$ m-des A_i, for any n

By quantificational logic this yields:

(K) $(\exists i)$ m-des $A_i \rightarrow (\forall i)$ m-des A_i [Compare (7) above]

This, clearly, is a way of saying that m-des is universalizable. And in adopting this principle we commit ourselves to the idea that moral desirability is *unconditional*—that what is morally right for the goose in the meadow is morally right for the gander in the farmyard.

This principle rules out the prospect of conflicts and dilemmas in the moral arena. A moral conflict will arise if A is m-des in some circumstance or condition and nevertheless not-A m-des in some other *co-realizible* circumstance or condition. In such a situation, both A and not-A could become morally indicated, thereby producing an overt clash. The way to avert this prospect is to stipulate that $(\exists i)$ m-des A_i precludes $(\exists i)$ not m-des A_i. And this comes down straightaway to (K) as indicated above.

Kant's generalization principle is accordingly tantamount to the exclusion of moral dilemmas in the just-indicated sense. As Kant sees it, moral desirability is thus acircumstantial (unconditional): what is *morally* desirable in one situation is so desirable in all situations. And this position has the consequence that no excuse can ever successfully exculpate an agent from doing the right thing—that if, for example, truth-telling is ever m-desirable at all, then it is m-desirable in every circumstance.

Note that, in virtue of the several implications affirmed above, it at once follows accepting (K) = (7m) constrains placing +'s throughout the c-row of the preceding implication table.

On Kantian principles, everything in the implication table *above* the last row (d-row) reads +. For a Kantian, m-desirability is accordingly subject to ground rules very different from those that hold desirability in general (and prudential desirability in particular), seeing that the m-denuded counterpart of thesis (K)—namely (7) above—obviously fails.

These considerations raise the question of whether, for a Kantian, (T1m) = (12m) will also obtain, so that concretization quandaries are also excluded. The answer is *No*. On the Kantian universalization principle (K) we do indeed obtain the m-versions of (7) - (9) above. But we do not obtain (T1m) = (12m) itself. Kant's unrealization principle (K) in and of itself rules out *conflict* dilemmas. But *concretization* dilemmas are not averted thereby.

To rid ourselves of concretization quandaries we would—additionally—need to adopt:

$$(T1m) = (12m) \qquad \text{m-des } (\exists i)\, A_i \to (\exists i)\, \text{m-des } A_i$$

And in fact, adopting any one of the trio (10m), (11m), (12m) would provide for the other two, and would thereby immunize us against concretization quandaries.

Thus in adopting (T1m) we at once obtain the result that +'s would obtain throughout the interaction table. *All* of those various modes of desirability (distributive/collective, conditional/generic) would simply coincide. In an ideal order, desirability is indivisible.

Here lies a useful lesson for understanding Kant's moral theory. It is often said that Kant's is an ideal-order morality. And this is indeed true. But the issue is somewhat complex. For, strictly speaking, an ideal order morality requires avoiding two different sorts of dilemmas:

(1) moral conflict dilemmas

(2) moral concretization dilemmas

A strong idealization morality accordingly calls for not just one generalization principle but two, namely:

(7m) $(\exists i)\, \text{m-des } A_i \to (\forall i)\, \text{m-des } A_i$

(11m) $\text{m-des } (\exists i)\, A_i \to \text{m-des } (\forall i)\, A_i$

The former guards against conflict dilemmas, the latter against moral concretization quandries. Distinct modes of unrealizability are involved: each principle requires something over and above the other. And Kantian K-universalizability in and of itself provides only for the first of them.

Would Kant also accept $(11m) = (T2)$? The answer lies in his 1793 essay "On the Dictum: That May Be So in Theory but Does Not Hold in Practice." Here he argues that "everything which is theoretically right in the *moral* domain must also be deemed appropriate in practice."[1] Thus anything that is deemed right and proper in the specifically moral sphere—that is, anything for which we have m-des $(\exists i)\ A_i$—must be accepted as morally right and proper in any and every co-instantiating case, so that m-des $(\forall i)\ A_i$. In the moral domain, so Kant insists the *abstractly* desirable is *universally* desirable. So here we do indeed have $(11m) = (T2)$.

The overall upshot is clear. Kant does indeed envision an idealization morality within whose aegis moral desirability is monolithic and indivisible. But this circumstance does *not* follow from his subscription to the universalization principle (K) alone; another mode of generalization is needed as well.

4. The Political Dimension

Let us now return from the somewhat rarified atmosphere of Kantian moral theory to the pragmatic level—and do so at what is the more mundane and crass level of politics. Here we confront the matter of people's desires—their preferences and choices based on self-interest (hopefully but not necessarily of the intelligently conceived sort).

The political arena is where the encounter with concretization quandaries are particularly common. There are innumerable cases in which the democratic process so operates that a social program or public work is generally acknowledged as something that is abstractly (or generically) desirable and desired, but where nevertheless each and every one of the concrete ways of realizing it is rejected. For the sake of a schematic example consider the following tabulation of favorable and unfavorable assessments.

Alternative Realization Modes	People's Evaluations				
	X_1	X_2	X_3	X_4	X_5
A_1	–	+	+	–	–
A $\quad A_2$	+	–	+	–	–
A_3	+	+	–	–	–
not-A	–	–	–	+	+

That A be realized in some way or other—i.e., $(\exists i)\ A_i$—is (so we here suppose) favored by most of those involved (viz., X_1-X_3, that is, 3 out of 5). Thus on the question A-somehow vs. not-A, a decided majority is in favor of A. But, equally, each and every one of the concrete ways of realizing A is opposed by a majority (likewise 3 out of 5). In such a situation our mini-society finds itself in a concretization quandary: there is no majoritatively acceptable way of reaching a majoritatively accepted goal.

Real-life instances are not hard to come by here. Indeed, we have here a situation that is only too common in democratic political contexts. Think of the common situation of a congressional stalemate or gridlock because there is on the one hand a virtually overwhelming public pressure—duly recognized in Congress—that something be done to resolve a problem but nevertheless each of the available resolutions is deemed unacceptable. (Consider, for example, the question devising of a tax scheme to pay for an urban development program where need is generally acknowledged.) In such situations, every *available* solution generates an opposition sufficiently powerful to defeat it. All too often in public affairs, a general acknowledgment and agreement that something be done to address a certain issue or resolve a certain problem is contrived with a widespread rejection of every available implementation. The result is a failure to abide by the plausible principle that "to will the end is to will the means" because each and every one of the means to that accepted end is itself deemed unacceptable.

Such concretization quandaries reflect the *logical* impossibility of adopting the (seemingly) nature principle of (seemingly) democratic process: *If the majority wants it done, then so be it—let it be done.* For in various cases the majority indeed wants A done, yet this can only be achieved by doing one or another of the A_i and the majority is against doing each and every one of the A_i. Thus consider the following situation:

Choice of Action		Individual Cost/Benefit Appraisal		
		X_1	X_2	X_3
	A_1	+	−	−
A	A_2	−	+	−
	A_3	−	−	+
	not-A	− −	− −	− −

Here − − indicates a *strong* negativity. All the individuals concerned favor $(\exists i)\ A_i$, so that there is unanimous agreement on A vs. not-A. But for each i, everyone except X_i opposes A_i, so that a majority would reject any particular A_i. The voting process results in "gridlocking" the universally favored measure A. (One sensible course in situations of this sort would be a random choice among the A_i which would (1) automatically assure realization of A, and (2) give to each party involved an equal chance of realizing its favored A_i. (Everyone is better off than with non-A. And in theory the gainers could somehow compensate the losers so as to secure their acquiescene.)

This example of random choice points to the need for (and potential availability of) mechanisms for resolving realization quandaries of the political sort. But it also points up the fact that these mechanisms can succeed only by putting the express choices of the parties involved into suspension. In such cases there is a need for an external resolution mechanism (the judiciary system?) to impose a solution on the gridlocked parties rather than trying to extract solutions from the overt preferences of the parties themselves.

5. SHIFT TO THE INTERNAL FORUM OF DELIBERATION

And of course much the same thing can happen *in foro interno* in the deliberations of single individual. Think of a situation much as before but now where the various "parties" involved are the factors at issue in the cost-benefit appraised— from different (equally weighty) value-perspectives—of the various actions at issue.

	Choice of Action	*Cost/Benefit Evaluation from a Certain Perspective*		
		P_1	P_2	P_3
A	A_1	-3	+2	+2
	A_2	+2	-3	+2
	A_3	+2	+2	-3
	not-A	-1	-1	-1

Looking at A_i generically (as a blurred amalgam) the aggregate value in each case is +1, which accordingly also holds true for A-as-a-whole and thereby renders it preferable to not-A. But nevertheless any particular A_i involves a negativity of -3 as regards the specific factor F_i, which could in the circumstances be sufficiently adverse to be unacceptable. (Thus, if we were concerned to maximize the minimum damage, not-A would be mandated here. And this would also be so if -2 represented a minimum floor of acceptability.) This sort of situation carries us back to cases of the sort considered at the outset of our discussion in connection with the examples of hapless process or the impoverished aristocrat. For what we have here is an instance of a not uncommon situation where each of the *available* routes (A_1–A_3) to an inherently desirable end (viz., avoidance of the negative -1 result inescapably associated with not-A) nevertheless themselves involve countervailing negativities (viz., the -3 result inescapably associated with each of the A_i). The desirability of the end is not sufficient to offset the negativities associated with the available means.

The lesson conveyed by the existence of cases of this sort is straightforward. With a concretization quandary the best course may well be to leave well enough alone. The princess might be best off staying home single with Daddy Ogre.

6. Pragmatic Anomalies

But was Kant right? Do moral precepts indeed generalize?

Pragmatic anomalies arise because it is wise on occasion to do something that seems foolish. They result from the fact that even appropriate rules can admit appropriate exceptions in practice. For there is, clearly, no conflict or contradiction on grounds of the general principles between the theses:

1. It is wise (advisable, prudent, appropriate, advantageous) *in general* to follow the rule *R*.

2. It is wise (advisable, prudent, appropriate, advantageous) *on occasion* to violate the rule *R*.

In general, even the best rules of practice will be subject to exceptions. And it is no less important to recognize the reverse point that exceptions require rules: there can be no exception where there is no rule and no excuse where there is no norm. (This side of the coin was somewhat neglected in John Austin's classic, "A Plea for Excuses.") It is in *this* sense that the classic dictum that the exception *proves* the rule must be construed. Exceptions have to be exceptions *to* something; it lies in the nature of things that they can only arise in the context of established norms.

On this perspective, it emerges that it is one thing to validate the appropriateness of a directive as a general rule of practice, and something rather different to establish that the rule must be obeyed in every case and, in particular, in the present case that is now before us. Generality is one thing and universality another where rules of action are concerned.

Our present concern is with something very different from violating a rule with a view to ulterior purposes. Consider the athlete who "throws the game" in order to win a bet or avert a threatened blackmail. Or again, consider the driver who exceeds the speed limit in order to rush an injured person to hospital. In such cases we have the situation of a general rule ("Play to win," "Drive legally") being set aside with a view to an overriding purpose introduced *ab extra* from outside the range of operation for which the rule was instituted (game competition or everyday driving). Here we make exception to the rule because some weightier purpose (financial gain or protecting life) intrudes upon the scene to overpower the aims and objectives that motivate the rule in question. This sort of thing will not concern us here. Rather, the focus of the present deliberations is with situations where there just is no rule-overriding domain-*exterior* overriding purpose outside the rule's own purposive orbit. Accordingly, the issue that primarily concerns us here is that of domain-*interior* rule-overriding considerations. Consider some examples of this phenomenon:

(1) The military technician who departs from a practice that sensible strategy would dictate in order to "throw his opponent off balance."

(2) The gambler who breaks the rules of good play deliber-

ately to keep from being predictable for the opposition in the interests of more effective gaming.

(3)   The artist or actor who breaks the rules "for effect"—to keep from being boring and escape from routine, i.e., to make the performance more entertaining.

Once we admit the cogency of such situations, we confront a significant context-specific limitation as regards the compellingness of otherwise appropriate rules.

What we have here is a breakdown of the principle of pragmatic universalization which stipulates:

(M)   Always do in each particular instance that which would be appropriate (would work out for the best) as a general practice—one that is duly stipulated in an appropriate rule.

As the preceding counterexamples indicate, this metarule is *not* a universally valid principle. It lays down a sensible rule—but one that itself admits of exceptions. The question accordingly arises: when *does* this rule hold? In what sorts of circumstances are exceptions admissable?

If it does not hold in general, then just when—that is, for what generic *class* of rules—does the metarule *M* hold good? And this confronts us with the further question: Are there any rules of praxis that hold with exception-precluding force?

Perhaps exceptionlessness arises with rules of a very high level of generality, such as "Do the prudentially appropriate thing." After all, one might think that if that "exception" were justifiable, then it would thereby, *ipso facto*, come to represent the prudentially appropriate thing. But this is not so. Think again of the military tactician who fails to do the prudentially right thing in order to "throw the opponent off balance." The point is that "the prudentially right thing" may itself become a problematic conception when a "higher prudence" has us cast *ordinary prudence* to the winds.

But what of something as generic and all-encompassing as "Do the morally right thing." Surely morality, unlike prudence, is sacrosanct. Surely a moral rule cannot be overriden! Or can it? To be sure, a whole series of moral theorists stretching from Immanuel Kant to Kurt Baier see the dictates of morality as all-predominant and inherently non-overridable. But is this indeed so?

We come here to a large and difficult issue. For example: Can a vast *prudential* advantage override a small *moral* transgression. (Could I defeasibly break my promise to meet you at a certain place and time when keeping it would—in the unforeseen circumstances—cost me a fortune?) Or can a great but nevertheless supererogatory benevolence override a small moral transgression. (Could I defensibly act—quite above and beyond the call of any duty—to assure a great (but otherwise unmerited) benefit for many at the cost of violating a sure trivially small commitment to someone)? Kant gave an emphatically negative answer. For him morality is categorically sacred with no transgressions—however small—admissible for any extenuous reasons. Moral rules (properly formulated) admit no exceptions. That makes moral acts universalizable, and indeed this universality—this principle that what is proper in a given case is proper always and exceptionlessly—is for Kant a key test of morality. But this position is deeply problematic. It runs against our moral intuitions that morality is a matter of *Fiat justitia ruat caelum*. It seems deeply problematic to insist that one must do the morally right thing though the heavens fall.

But the issue can be made to assume a somewhat different aspect. Consider what is ordinarily thought of as a moral rule—for example, "Do not inflict pain!" But what of doctors and dentists who do inflict pain, but only in the patients' best interests. Kant had a cagy strategy for circumventing this difficulty—that of building the *motive* into the characterization of the action at issue. "Do not harm others just for your own pleasure." "Do not inflect needless pain on others." Insofar as motivation is pivotal for morality this seems to make for categorical rules. Kant's idea was that properly formulated moral rules—or "maxims" as he called them—will themselves involve specifying the motive/reason for the action and thereby preclude exceptions, seeing that there will now be no prospect of a "conflict of rules" or of "overriding considerations." This Kantian strategy is to all appearances an effective and serviceable strategy for arriving at nonoverridable rules.

But of course what makes these Kantian rules or "maxims" exceptionless is that it lies in the nature of the case that the exception must look not just to action but also to motivation. (It is not "Do not kill" that is the rule, but "Do not murder," and not "Do not hurt people" but "Do not hurt people simply for your own pleasure.") And this is, in a way, cheating. Because the resultant rules will be not just rules of action (behavior) but rather rules of motivation proceeding with reference to what is to go on imperceptably in an agent's mind, confined to the internal form of thought's thought.

Yet what if we insist on looking for rules of *overt action* in the public forum—rules governing the sort of agent comportment that can be observed and perceived by others? At this point we would concentrate our focus upon matters of overt behavior and observable praxis, putting aside all matters of unobservable plans, purposes, and intentions by focusing upon what people actually and overtly *do*. Are there any exception-precluding ("unbreakable") rules here?

One plausible place to look in the effort to get at such unbreakable rules is in a very different domain of praxis, namely games. Take chess rules for example. "Always move bishops diagonally." Such a rule is exception-precluding simply because any *seeming* violation takes us outside the realm of reality (viz., chess-playing) for which the rule is apposite. This clearly is an "unbreakable" and thus exception-precluding rule. Of course it is not *physically* impossible to move the bishop otherwise, but it is impossible within the framework of the game. For if one were to violate this rule one would, *ipso facto*, no longer be playing chess. Here we come to the important difference between game-defining rules vs. rules of strategy, seeing that breaking the rule means not playing at all rather than merely not playing well.

And we find yet another context that is substantially similar to this games-playing situation in the case of mathematics. Consider the rules: "Do not divide by zero," or "Do not come up with 5 when multiplying 2 by 2." Such rules too are unexceptionable—not in that incompetents cannot make mistakes, but rather in that in breaking such rules one is no longer playing the arithmetic game.

The point is that, with any project whose very nature is defined (as per chess or arithmetic) by rules that provide for definitionally rigid constituting specifications, it will be impossible, in the very nature of things, at one and the same time to violate the rules and to continue functioning within the enterprise at issue. With any such conventional practice, the rules in effect constitute that practice as the thing it is. But prudence and morality are not like that. They are enterprises that root not in *conventions* but in the requirements of human life (achieving our purposes, interacting appropriately with our fellows, etc.).

The difference between a nature-mandated and an artifical mode of praxis is thus crucial for the purposes of the present considerations. The rules of an artificial (artefactual, man-made) activity such as games-playing (chess) or symbol mongering (speaking German) or mathematical manipulation (arithmetic) can afford to be practice-definitive—and thereby preemptory and unsolvable—because if you violate the rules you are out of the practice and you can chose to do this. For artificial practices, unlike in natural ones (breathing, eating), are *optional*: you can chose simply not to engage in them. But those nature-mandated ones are not. Accordingly the former (optional) practices can manage to have unexceptionable rules of the violate-the-rules-and-you-are-out-of-the-practice-type. But the letter (mandatory) practices cannot manage this, seeing that the practice is inescapable, as it were: one just can't extract oneself from it. The rules of games, in short, can afford to be practice-defining and exception-precluding, but the rules of life (and thus of prudence and morality and cogent reasoning) cannot afford to do so.

7. THE FACTS OF LIFE

Life is holistic. Its teleological structure of needs and wants is complex, many-sidedly systemic; its components and aspects are symbiotically interrelated. It has no place for unbending rigidities. It is not conventional but natural. And so its departments are not autonymous (separable, hermetically sealed) and compartmentizable but rather symbiotically interconnected. They are organically interactive. What goes on in one can be affected—and eventually offset—by what goes on elsewhere. The rules of here may have to give way to the demands of there.

The rules of practice in life—of prudence, morality, etiquette, etc., do not fall into hermetically sealed compartments. They are not rules of an artificial, conventional praxis that is purposively self-maintained. And so, in the praxis of life and its major departments—prudence and morality included—pragmatic anomalies can always arise. In the praxis of life, all rules have their exception—though, of course, this circumstance neither destroys the validity of those rules as rules, nor does it abrogate the need to respect them for what they are. The trouble with Kant's ethics lies in its commitment to those very idealization principles that we examined earlier on. A moral doctrine designed for strong idealization principles that we examined at the outset. A moral doctrine designed for operation in the real world cannot appropriately hitch its wagon to the stern of idealization to that extent.

The ultimate point can be put simply:

(1)　Those mandating practices of human life are so diversified/complex that there are always external considerations.

(2)　Hence exceptions can always arise.

(3)　Hence pragmatic anomalies can always arise.

In life—unlike games—the rules are made to be broken. But never, of course, frivolously—otherwise those rules would not be what they are. Exceptions will generally arise. But they will only do so appropriately when they are rooted in cogent and sufficient reasons. To *this* rule there are no exceptions.

Note

1. *Op. cit.*, sect. I, *ad fin.*

Chapter Eight

REICHENBACH FALLS
(OR ONLY STUMBLES?)

REICHENBACH, PROBABILITY, AND THE
PROBLEM OF SURPLUS MEANING

1. INTRODUCTION

THERE is no question but that Hans Reichenbach developed
one of the most systematic, complex, and sophisticated phi-
losophies of knowledge propounded in the twentieth century.
He is, after all, the author and exponent of a highly interesting
and influential program in probabilistic epistemology. The present paper, however, will focus upon what seems to be a rather
deep and far-reaching defect in Reichenbach's overall approach
—an intrinsic maladjustment or incoherence in his epistemology.
For the problem is that of whether two of its main components—
the theory of empirical knowledge with the theory of probability—are mutually coherent and compatible.

2. REICHENBACH'S THEORY OF EMPIRICAL KNOWLEDGE

Reichenbach was first and foremost, an empiricist. For him,
our knowledge of matters of fact roots ultimately in the deliverances of sense: in the phenomena that we can observe by sensory means. As he saw it, our knowledge of the world's facts
starts with the actual sensory observations of individual people, pivoting on what he calls "phenomenal reports," by whose
means sensory observations are formulated. We humans only
have *immediate cognitive access* to personal observations—as
conveyed in those "phenomenal reports"—and have no cognitive access to the actual physical states that they represent that
bypasses observation. Our knowledge of objective fact is always experientially based.

But no less fundamental to Reichenbach's theory of knowledge is an acute awareness of the gap between personal experi-

ence and objective fact. The move from experiential observation to objective fact requires crossing a deep cognitive divide. Reichenbach emphasized that statements of *objective fact* inevitably have a "surplus of meaning" that outruns the reach of observational surveillance. Statements about everyday-life concreta (tables and chairs) or theoretical/explanatory entities (atoms and molecules) always have observation-transcending implications and ramifications. The assertive content of their substantive claims reaches far beyond the phenomenal reports that provide their evidential basis and grounding. Objective factual claims have retrodictive and predictive ramifications that reach beyond anything we can actually get hold of in actual experience. No volume of claims about what people do or can see, or hear, or feel, etc., can exhaust the assertive content of the claim: "That is a duck waddling along over there." Accordingly, statements about the objective physical situation can never be reduced to mere compounds or complexes of experience-reporting sense-impression statements. Objective factual claims involve more than observational phenomenology.

In consequence of this evidence-transcendence, we can never be in an epistemic position to regard our physical object statements being as *certain*. Reichenbach accordingly launches a far-flung attack on empirical certainty. In particular he unweighed against the "observational certainty" of his positivist colleagues, decisively rejecting the idea that statements about the objective world are somehow an aggregative construction (*Aufbau*) from *Protokollsätze* that supposedly provide us with altogether certain facts about the world. And he also energetically opposed C. I. Lewis' direct observational truths—the "so-called terminating statements." As Reichenbach saw it, the step from our phenomenal experiences and sensory impressions on the one hand, to claims about what we actually see (that is an apple or a duck) is never immediate and automatic. A factual observation report ("I see a duck") is always to some extent conjectural and thus defeasible and less than certain. Because phenomenal claims always fall short in asserted content in relation to claims regarding objective reality, we do not actually observe concrete real-world objects as such, that is "not as they objectively are, but in a disturbed form: we see a *substitute world* [of sense objects perceived 'from the standpoint of our middle-sized dimensions']—not the [physical] world as it is, objectively speaking" (*Experience and Prediction* [1938], p. 220).

Experience relates to a stand-in substitute domain—a realm of what we would nowadays call *virtual* reality—that cannot be identified with physical reality as such.

As Reichenbach saw it, the step from empirical observation to fact can only be accomplished by means of *probabilistic* relationships. We cannot move from experience to fact directly, seeing that there is no sense-certainty. Nor yet can we do so inferentially (as phenomenalists would have it). Rather, we can only proceed *probabilistically*. This recourse to probabilism lay at the heart and core of Reichenbach's theory of empirical knowledge.

Take our duck as a somewhat frivolous example. The observed data—those looks, waddles, quacks—don't *constitute* the duck; and they don't *imply* the duck either by providing some sort of assured guarantee of its existence. For Reichenbach, the observed data merely give *probabilistic evidence* for something that has objective reality. And so, for Reichenbach, the theory of empirical/observational knowledge runs out into the theory of probability. For him, the gap between appearance and reality, between empirical experience and objective fact can only be crossed by *probabilistic* means.

3. REICHENBACH'S THEORY OF PROBABILITY

This brings us to Reichenbach's theory of probability. Its salient features for our present purposes are that, according to Reichenbach, probability—

1. is basically statistical (i.e., involves a "frequency interpretation")

2. deals with objective relations among specific real-world events. (He does *not* have a psychological, personalist subjectionistic conception of probability.)

3. is based on a probability relation that involves a coordination among what Reichenbach calls *event sequences*—i.e., chronological series of "events" in the aforementioned sense.

The whole structure of Reichenbach's theory of probability is accordingly based upon his fundamental formula: "The probability statement is a general implication between statements concerning a class membership of the elements of certain *given* sequences." As he sees it, any meaningful probability-number determination rests on our capacity to make event-instantiation determinations in concrete given cases. For these alone can provide the statistical record on which probability-claims have to be based.

4. THE ISSUE OF SINGLE-CASE DETERMINATIONS

But now comes a difficulty. How can such single-case determinations of objective fact possibly be made? How—for example—can we ascertain that this present particular event is one of "seeing a duck." How—that is—can we possibly validate, on Reichenbachian principle, the claim that the objective item that is presently at issue actually really is—in the particular case at hand—a genuine duck? This, after all, is something we have to do if we are to assess (via a statistical record of past experience) that a certain particular value is appropriate for the probability of the implication: "If you apprehend what looks like a duck, waddles like a duck, and quacks like a duck then it *is* a duck." The development of correlation statistics requires us to establish that (in various instances) a particular assessment of the situation is objectively correct. And this is where the difficulty roots.

To use the calculus of probabilities we must obtain probability-values. And to obtain a usable probability-value we must establish statistics—that is to do numerical counting of the occurrence of real-world events. But if we are to be able to do statistics, to do actual-instantiation counting—as we must if we are ever to be in a position to make probability assignments—then we must be in a position to determine just exactly when and where A-membership has been associated with B-membership with respect to event-classes. And this calls for our being able to make determinations that in this or that particular case of A-membership, B-membership is or is not co-present. Probability-evaluations have to root in particular case determinations.

Yet how, on Reichenbach's own principles, is such an event-instantiation determination to be made?

Clearly, once we abandon the idea of an experiential sure-thing determination, an observational certainty, *this will itself have to be done by probabilistic means.* But what sorts of probabilistic resources does Reichenbach provide for us to effect single-case judgments of probability?

The interesting and crucial consideration in this context is that Reichenbach's theory of probability provides one and only one probabilistic mechanism that authorizes us to make categorical judgments about single cases, namely what Reichenbach calls a *posit*. As Reichenbach puts it (in *The Theory of Probability*): "A posit is a statement with which we deal as true, although the truth value is [actually] unknown." But the only basis of rational justification for making such a posit, as far as Reichenbach is concerned, is a high probability of the fact at issue. And this high probability in a particular case must itself root in generality—i.e., must be grounded in this case being one of a class for which a high probability can be obtained. What is at issue here is a cognitive *transfer* of that high generality-coordinate probability to the particular case at issue.

It is exactly this stratagem of cognitive transfer that underlies what Reichenbach calls the "fictitious meaning" of single-case probability statements: "The statement concerning the probability of a single case...is given a *fictitious meaning*, constructed by a transfer of meaning from the general to the particular" (*ibid.*). When a fact can be represented as highly probable it can be posited or postulated as actual by an act of intellectual fiat, as it were. But such a fiat itself can only be validated probabilistically. *To make Reichenbachian posits we already need probabilities.*

5. The Problem

And exactly here lies the problem. For Reichenbach, probability-determinations require the compilation of individual case statistics, but individual-case determinations are parasitic on general-probability appraisals.

The situation stands as follows. We can, according to Reichenbach's stipulations, posit "This X is a Y" only on the basis of the consideration that:

(1) This X is a Y with high probability, because

(2) In appropriately similar cases, X's have been Y's, with a probability well in excess of 1/2.

But the establishment of (2) itself calls for statistics of the format:

(3) In case i, X (namely X_i) has generally been a Y (namely Y_i).

And, as Reichenbach has it, the determination of such individual-case situations is itself something that has to be determined probabilistically. The whole approach accordingly founders on the fact that in the attempt to measure one probability, we are driven back to determine yet another.

Reichenbach the empiricist insists that we can only reach objective facts from the relevant experiential reports. Only from our experience "that something looks, waddles, and quacks like a duck" can we effect the epistemic transit to "it is a duck." And on Reichenbach's principles this transition requires correlation statistics. We have to be able to move from statistics for past cases of various instances of

duck-like phenomena

to past encounters with

actual ducks.

And this means that in these *past* cases—those past *individual* cases—we must establish the presence of actual ducks.

But if this is so, then all we have managed to accomplish is to transpose the issue from the present into the yet more problematic past. For what we have done is to move from establishing

it is a duck (here, now)

to

it was a duck (on sundry past occasions).

Here then, we come to a deep—and to all appearances insuperable—problem in Reichenbach's theory of knowledge. For Reichenbach:

- Fact determination (in matters of objective fact) is always cognitively parasitic on probability assessments.

- Probability assessments are always cognitively parasitic on established (and thus past-tensedly accomplished) fact determinations.

And it is clear that we are going to confront an insuperable difficulty in any attempt to put these pieces together.

6. THE DIFFICULTY

One further important consideration is in order. In a lucid and illuminating lecture entitled "Are Phenomenal Reports Absolutely Certain?" (*Phil. Rev.*, vol. 61 [1952], pp. 147-59), Reichenbach argues that for him probability statements need not set certainties, in the sense that the statement "The probability of event E is p" need not itself be taken to have probability 1. We can—meaningfully and self-consistently—see real higher level probabilistic statements as themselves merely having some probability or other, rather than being true outright.

And this reasoning is perfectly correct. But it is beside the point of the present objection and affords no comfort in the context of the presently envisioned problem. For the problem for present purposes is that of the question:

> What would one have to know or presuppose or posit in order to be in an epistemic position (on Reichenbach's own principles) to determine that "The probability of E is p?"

And the answer is that one would then have to preestablish or presuppose or posit a whole series of other probabilistic facts. Somewhat picturesquely put, Reichenbach's epistemology puts us into a situation reminiscent of Zeno's paradox: before taking that first probabilistic step we would be to take another step before which we would have to take yet another probabilistic step, and so on.

7. THE DILEMMA

It now becomes clear that an internal incoherence or incongruity lies deep within Reichenbach's epistemology. For when we put the various pieces together, we see that we have to face the problem that probability numbers can only be obtained from real-event statistics ("This is a red ball I have drawn for the urn," or "This is the track of a particle issuing from disintegration of a uranium atom"). To obtain such statistics we must make event-determinations ("having a red ball in hand; seeing a uranium atom disintegration on our sensors). But in making such single-event determinations we already need—on Reichenbachian principles—to have in hand a preestablished probability to authorize a posit. As it stands, Reichenbach's epistemology can only be implemented if we have probability numbers at our disposal, and when it comes to securing such numbers we realize that we have no nonprobabilistic way to get there from here.

Reichenbach's epistemology is thus driven into a very tight corner from which it cannot emerge without major modification. For in confronting the problem of making probability-determinations, Reichenbach faces a choice between:

Either (1) to allow observational certitude, contrary to his theory of knowledge. This would resolve the problem of the vicious regress of having probabilities be based on probabilities that must themselves be based on more fundamental probabilities, and so on "all the way down."

Or (2) to abandon the probabilistically based posit approach to individual-case judgments and allow for an inference of some nonprobabilistic sort from observation to a probability judgment (from "it looks, waddles, and quacks like a duck," to "it probably is a duck" as a step that is itself possible without probabilistic mediation).

Reichenbach faces a difficult choice. He can either readjust his theory of knowledge to the needs and requirements of his theory of probability, or, the other way around, can readjust his theory of probability to his theory of observational knowledge. But what he cannot have, it would seem, is an unmodified epistemology that allows the internal incoherence or incongruity of his overall epistemology to stand unresolved.[1]

Note

1. This chapter is a revised version of a paper contributed to a conference held in 1992 in Hamburg, Germany to celebrate the centennial of Reichenbach's birth.

Chapter Nine

CHISHOLM'S ONTOLOGY OF THINGS

IN view of the inherent interest and the wide influence of his philosophizing, it is well worthwhile to scrutinize closely Roderick Chisholm's ontological position regarding substances and their origination. A promising strategy here is to proceed by throwing a clearer light on the inherent presumptions and presuppositions of Chisholm's treatment of the issues. The methodology will be that of a contrast case comparison. Following up Chisholm's own comparison between his substance-metaphysic and an alternative process-oriented metaphysic, our discussion will try to bring to clearer view his basic assumptions regarding the metaphysical lay of the land.

With Chisholm, substances may undergo changes of (or in) their properties, but such changings are not themselves *properties* of things—though they are "attributes" in the wider sense of being correctly attributable in discourse about them (p. 103).[1] The cardinal defect of process metaphysics—from Chisholm's point of view—lies in its view that all true assertions that are (seemingly) about things and their attributes root in (emerge from, are reducible to supervene upon—as you prefer) matters that lie outside the category of good old honest things and their properties—namely in states and affairs and their changes and continuities. The only "events" that are ontologically respectable for Chisholm are alterations in the properties of things (or of "sums of things," p. 152). Attributes or changes that do not represent properties of things, thing-complexes, or pseudo-things ("the social or economic *system*") are dismissed by him as being somehow suspect—perhaps even occult.

Given his commitment to substances as traditionally conceived, Chisholm's treatment of coming into being and passing away pivots on these theses:

1. What exists—and *all* that exists—are things (substances) and their descriptive features (properties, relations). Accordingly, apart from the origination and termination of substances themselves, the only sort of change that there is is an

alteration in their properties and relations, in the descriptive (*secundum quid*) condition of substances.

2. Consequently, existing persons—"you and I—are real things, *entia realia*." In fact, for Chisholm persons represent the quintessential or paradigm substances.

3. Things in general, and persons in particular, must come into (and go out of) existence all at once. They cannot originate gradually, initiating through a process of some sort. For to accept this would be to hold of something that there was a time when it did not fully exist—a juncture at which it did not and yet somehow did exist—which is absurd. If a thing is available to do anything whatsoever—emerging into existence included—then it must actually exist then and there.

4. Hence while persons might change over time in point of their properties, their relations, and even their mode of existence—say in their individual development from a subhuman status of some sort into full-fledged *human* beings—they cannot change over time from nonbeings to beings (from nonexistents to existents):

> I am certain, then, that this much is true: that if I am a real thing and not just a *façon de parler*, then neither my coming into being nor my passing away is a gradual process—however gradual may be my entrance into and my exit from the class of *human* beings [my entrance into or exit from the class of beings (of existents) must be abrupt and instantaneous]. (P. 59.)

For Chisholm, as for Aristotle, origination (*genesis*) is something altogether different from change (*metabolē*).

5. In consequence substances cannot undergo change of identity. One substance cannot possibly ever change into another. The closest we could possibly get to this would be the origination of one substance following instantaneously on the termination of another, descriptively and spatial-temporally related one.

As these considerations indicate, Chisholm's metaphysical stance is that substance-origination must be instantaneous: there is an instant prior to which the substance as such never existed and after which the substance always exists up to some subsequent time of its expiry.

It is clear, however, that such instantaneous origination is not the only theoretically available possibility. An alternative view would contemplate the prospect of an interval of concrescence—a noninstantaneous emergence into existence. This alternative model would see origination as a *process*, envisioning a gestation period between nonexistence and existence—an interval during which the thing at issue comes into being, that is, literally emerges into existence. And if coming-into-being is genuinely a process, then there has to be a juncture of transition —of reification or concrescence—during which it can neither be said truly that the thing at issue actually exists nor on the other hand that it does not exist at all.[2] This contrasting way of looking at the matter of origination characterizes the position of such process philosophers as, for example, A. N. Whitehead.

Three salient facts must be noted about such an interval of substance-origination:

1. It is a "fuzzy" interval that has no definite, specifiable temporal beginning or end.

2. During this interval we can say neither that the thing (already) exists nor that it does not (yet) exist; during the gestation period the substance's existence is *indeterminate*.

3. If the world had been annihilated during this interval, then it would neither be correct to say that the thing has (ever) existed in the world nor that it has not (ever) existed. The theses that the thing has existed (at some time or other) would also have to be classified as indeterminate. (From the ontological point of view it could be said that, figuratively speaking, the world "has not managed to make up its mind" about the existence of the thing. The world itself is, in this regard, indeterminate.)

As these observations make all too clear, a rigorous implementation of the idea of reification as a process—of a thing's coming into existence over a course of time—requires the deployment of two distinctly unorthodox items of concept-machinery:

i. a "fuzzy logic"—or at any rate a fuzzy mathematics—that puts the conception of indefinite (imprecisely bounded) intervals and regions at our disposal.[3]

ii. a semantics of truth-value gaps, serving to countenance propositions that are neither (definitely) true nor (definitely) false but indeterminate in lacking a classical truth-value.[4]

Neither of these unorthodoxies is inherently absurd; both represent theoretical resources that are today well known and widely employed in logic and in the theory of information management. (Indeed, the second idea goes back all the way to Aristotle himself—in the sea battle example of the discussion of future contingency in Chapter 9 of *De interpretatione*.)

From this vantage point, Chisholm's position emerges into a clearer light. In particular, the following choices lie before us in the context of ontological theorizing:

1. Whether to adopt an ontology of substances (things) or one of processes (state-changes):

	Item	Aspect	Connection Between Aspect & Item
Substance Account	thing	property or relation	belongs to, characterizes
Process Account	process	subprocess	part/whole (processually interpreted)

2. Whether to adopt a logic (and mathematics) that is descriptively hard-edged and binary or one that countenances fuzzy boundaries.

3. Whether to adopt a semantics that is classically bivalent or one that countenances indeterminate propositions which lack a classical truth-value (true or false).

Chisholm's approach is based on certain particular choices that are not altogether explicit in his discussion, but seem to issue from the idea that only one workable course is available to sensible people. However, the actual situation is more complex and ambiguous.

Chisholm's position reflects a deeply conservative, classical world-view in which there is no room for process ontology, fuzzy logic, and a semantics of truth-value indeterminacy. It involves an undefended and indeed even largely unstated commitment to a classicism which, though widely shared, is certainly not so urgently compelling that sensible people cannot but go along. Our hand is not forced in matters of ontological systematization to the extent that his treatment of the issues would indicate. The fact is that we do have alternatives—each associated with certain costs and benefits, certain assets and liabilities.

Chisholm's restrictively conservative view of the nature of coming to be and passing away of things also colors his position on the issue of substantial change. For Chisholm is em-

CHISHOLM'S ONTOLOGY / 141

phatic that one substance cannot change into another (as a caterpillar might transform into a butterfly) or two substances unite to form a third (as two corporations might merge to start a new one). To say that x has changed into y is for Chisholm absurd—a simply flawed formulation of the idea that one ongoing substance z has changed from an x-condition to a y-condition. For Chisholm, any purported mutation of substance-identity must be glossed as a change in some substance-descriptive condition. As he sees it, all change is alteration, change in the descriptive, *secundum quid* condition of substances.

However the pivotal *argument* that Chisholm gives for this rejection of identity-change is deeply problematic. It runs as follows:

> Suppose there is something, say the G that is identical with the H today and will be diverse from the H tomorrow. If the H is now identical with the G, then anything that is [now] true of the G is also [now] true of the H. Therefore if the G will be diverse from the H tomorrow, then the H will be diverse from the H tomorrow. But this consequence is absurd. (P. 55)

It is clear that this reasoning has its problems. If we are going to bring time and change into the orbit of our deliberations, then we have to be careful about keeping track of our time indices properly adjusted throughout. Thus let $T_t(p)$ = "it is true at time t that p," and let n = now = today. Then Chisholm's argument runs as follows:

(1) $T_n (G = H)$	by supposition
(2) $T_n + 1 (G \neq H)$	by supposition
(3) As of n = now: $G = H$	from (1)
(4) $T_n + 1 (H \neq H)$	from (2) via (3) by identity substitution

Now (4) is indeed absurd. But of course its derivation depends upon *combining* (2) and (3), a step which is, in the circumstances, clearly inappropriate in its mixing of temporal indices. Chisholm's reasoning is in fact question begging since it hinges a recourse to the thesis: "once identical is always identical," which is exactly what is in question. In the temporal contexts all attributions of properties and relationships must be time-qualified, identity relationships included.

There may considerably be some plausible metaphysical reasons why identity-changes in substances should not be contemplated. But this would have to be established explicitly on substantive metaphysical grounds. It would be quite unrealistic to expect—with Chisholm—that mere logic as such should put this sort of metaphysically substantive conclusion at our disposal.

Chisholm's implicit commitment to a position of "once identical always identical" again betokens a very conservative perspective—a commitment to an emphatically classical perspective that leaves out of sight the complexities introduced by the emergence of modern tense logic as an alternative approach.

One could, of course, envision a definitional strategy to omnitemporalize identity. That is, one could insist on a construction of identity that assures:

$$G = H \text{ iff } (\forall t) \, T_t \, (G = H)$$

On this basis we would have it that $T_t \, (G = H)$ iff $T_{t'} \, (G = H)$, for any t, t'. Identity now becomes a sempiternal, time-irrelevant relationship rather than one that is (like so much else in this world) transitory and changeable. But of course this is something that cannot simply be assumed. It must be argued directly—over and above any purely logical considerations. It represents an overt *decision* about the way in which we propose to construct our temporal logic and semantics. It represents one particular choice within a range of theoretically available alternatives. And so it is not something that one theorist can simply impose on another. Accordingly, Chisholm's denial of any prospect of changes in identity is yet another deeply problematic aspect of his substantialistic metaphysic.

It is unquestionably true that the ontological bias of Western philosophy since the days of Aristotle has run in favor of things (substances). Within the ambience of this bias, those metaphysicians who have not altogether denied the reality of process and change (as did Parmenides and F. H. Bradley) have generally sought to minimize its role. And Chisholm stands squarely in this tradition. For, abstractly speaking, one can contemplate process and change as operating at somewhat different ontological levels:

1. processes of change in the *properties of things*

2. processes of change in the *existence of things*

    (a) coming to be and passing away (i.e., change in point of existence) as a process

    (b) change of identity as a process

3. processes of changes in *states of affairs* independently of things (and their properties and relations).

Now, to be sure, Chisholm is not Parmenides. He is prepared to acknowledge the occurrence of genuine change in relation to the properties of things. But this is as far as he is willing to go: he refuses to move beyond level 1. And the *reason* for this (as apart from any philosophically extraneous issues of *motive*) lies ultimately—as best I can see—in the domain of logic and semantics. Chisholm sees himself as impelled to his position by inexorable logical and semantical considerations. But as the preceding considerations have suggested, this stance is in the final analysis deeply problematic. It is questionable precisely because of the narrowness of Chisholm's logico-semantical traditionalism—his reluctance to move beyond the classical sector of the domain.

It may be, of course, that such a traditionalism is the way not just of conservatism but also of wisdom. Conceivably, leaving the straight and narrow path of logico-semantical traditionalism leads ultimately to difficulties and obstacles that make the price of our newfound freedoms too steep. But this, surely, is something that has to be established explicitly and in great detail before one could be justified in forgoing the rich resources and opportunities of these fertile innovations.

To bring the issue into a more concrete focus, let us consider one particular ontological problem: that of a *gappy* existence. Here we contemplate the prospect of an individual whose history involves lapsing from existence. On such a view of "intermittent existence," the substance at issue vanishes for a time into an ontological tunnel—as it were—from which it emerges, the same item as before, after a certain interval of nonexistence. Such a situation is easy to describe, though not easy to illustrate in the world's ordinary course of physical things existing at a level of scale above that of subatomic particles. On the other hand, legal entities (nations, corporations, publication series, and the like, afford numerous illustrations of entities that can display the phenomenon of intermittent existence. Here Chisholm avails himself of the convenient recourse of dismissing the sense of identity at issue when one claims that "the thing that existed before the lapse is identically the same thing as the thing that which exists after the lapse" as being "loose and popular" in contrast to "strict and philosophical."[5] But this dismissal is, surely, little more than tendentious invective. The actual situation seems to be one of there being two different constructions of "is the same thing that existed before"—a less restrictive one that permits interruptions, and a more restrictive one that precludes them. And nothing in the abstract nature of things logical or metaphysical dictates that one must grant to continuous existence a status somehow *superior* to that of intermittent existence.

At this point, we came to Chisholm's treatment of the "Ship of Theseus" problem of the vessel rebuilt over time plank by plank, yet with those old planks saved up and eventually reassembled. (Is the resultant vessel still the actual Ship of Theseus?) This example points beyond the question of *interrupted* existence to encompass also the problem of a *divided* existence. Chisholm's position here is as follows:

> When the existence of such a borderline case does thus require us to make a choice between "Yes" and "No," the decision is an entirely pragmatic one, simply a matter of convenience.... The important thing here is this: The convention of the courts, or of the proper authorities will settle the matter.... It would make no sense to say: Well, it just might be, you know, that they are mistaken. (Pp. 32-33)

Chisholm thus draws a clear line. With questions of *descriptive* sameness of the form "Is it the same *X*?" (the same ship, the same stocking), we have the "loose and popular" sense of sameness/identity, and the situation here is one of a conventional decision—though not necessarily an arbitrary one, but one that is pragmatically based on contextual convenience. But with a question of *substantial* sameness, "Is it the same item?" (the same thing, the same object) encounter the "strict and philosophical sense of sameness," and the situation is seen as one of factual correctness based on the ontological/semantical realities which—as Chisholm has it—preclude eccentricities along the lines of interruptions and splittings.

However, Chisholm's insistence that there is a night-and-day difference between the two cases raises three problems:

1. Just what is it about *substantial* sameness (the same thing) that sets it so sharply and categorically apart from *descriptive* sameness (the same ship) that the former is something "strict and philosophical" while the latter remains merely "loose and popular"? In particular—

2. Why is it that descriptive sameness is "merely pragmatic" while substantial sameness is something hard and fast? Why

should one not take the line that sameness/identity is prag-matic "all the way down," ruled by considerations of proce-dural convenience just as much in substantive as in descriptive cases?

3. Even granting for the sake of discussion that substantial sameness ("the same thing") is something hard-and-fast dis-tinguishable for descriptive sameness ("the same ship"), why is it that person-sameness ("the same person") should be assimilated to strict substantial rather than to loose de-scriptive sameness?

The impetus of such questions indicates that Chisholm's posi-tion is far more problematic than his own discussion would give one any reason to suspect.

This carries us back to Chisholm's perspective of seeing persons as paradigm things (substances). And one is entitled to ask: What Ptolemaic verity is it that puts us humans at the cen-ter of the ontological universe? Why see people, rather, say, than atoms, as quintessential substances? After all, there is no reason of fundamental principle why persons themselves could not or should not be conceptualized in other, nonsubstantival terms (and especially as processes). And at this juncture we come to Chisholm's critique of the process approach (pp. 94-95).

The fact is that process philosophy does not evoke much interest or sympathy for Chisholm. He dismisses it in one brief paragraph:

> There are "process"-philosophers who say that such things as human bodies and matchbooks are really processes. But, so far as I know, no one has ever devoted any philosophical toil to showing how to *reduce* such things to processes. In the ab-sence of such a reduction, I would agree with C. D. Broad...: "It is plainly contrary to common sense to say that the phases in the history of a thing are parts of the thing." ...[A former per-son] is an individual who once had the shape and size of a man, but no process or career can have the shape and size of a man. (Pp. 94-95)

These dismissive remarks afford a far-reaching indication of the basis for and motivation of Chisholm's ontological position. For Chisholm, the idea of persons as processes is a metaphysical horror. He is unwilling to take seriously the prospect that tradi-tional physical objects—let alone persons!—should be under-stood in terms of something as inherently temporal and transitory as processes. But in the light of this negativism, his position does process philosophy less than justice.

Chisholm sees the issue of persons and their identity as his ace in the hole. His commitment to a substances-geared ontology is to all available appearances heavily motivated by a conviction that persons and their identity can be understood, and can *only* be appropriately understood, through concerning of them as substantial things. But this qualifies as a rather dubious proposition.

If one is committed to conceiving of a *person* within the framework of a classical thing-metaphysic, then one is going to be impelled inexorably towards the materialist view that the definitive feature of a person is his body and its doings, this being the only readily available person-relative item that is readily conceptualized as a thing, seeing that, of everything that appertains to us, it is clearly one's *body* that is most readily and apprehensibly assimilated to the substance paradigm.[6] Think here of David Hume's ventures into self-apprehension:

> From what (experiential) impression could this idea [of *self*] be derived? This question is impossible to answer without a manifest contradiction and absurdity; and yet it is a question which must necessarily be answered, if we would have the idea of self pass for clear and intelligible. …For my part, when I enter most intimately into what I call *myself*, I always stumble on some particular perception or other, of heat or cold, light or shade, love or hatred, pain or pleasure. I never can catch *myself* at any time without a perception, and never can observe anything but the perception.[7]

Surely Hume is perfectly right here. Any such quest for *observational* confrontation with a personal core substance, a self or ego that constitutes the particular person that one is, is destined to end in failure. The only "things" about ourselves that we—and others—can get hold of *observationally* is the body and its activities and sensations. But is this where we really want to place our bets or regard the issue of personal identity? After all, it feels decidedly uncomfortable to conceptualize *people* (persons) as *things* (substances)—oneself above all—because we resist flat-out identification with our bodies. Aristotle already bears witness to this difficulty of accommodating the self or soul into a substance-metaphysic. It is, he tells us, the "substantial form," the *entelechy* of the body. But this accommodation strategy raises more problems than it solves, because the self or soul is so profoundly unlike the other sorts of entelechy-examples that Aristotle is able to provide.

The self or ego has always been a stumbling-block for Western philosophy because of its resistance to accommodation within its favored framework of substance-ontology. The idea that "the self" is a *thing* (substance)—and that whatever takes place in "my mind" and "my thoughts" is a matter of the activity of a thing of a certain sort (a "mind"-substance)—is surely no more than a rather blatant sort of fiction—a somewhat desperate effort to apply the "thing" paradigm to a range of phenomena that it just doesn't fit.

The fact is that people instinctively dislike being described in thing-classificatory terms. As Sartre indicates, a wrongdoer may be prepared to say "I did this or that act" but will resist saying "I am a thief," "I am a murderer."[8] Such attributions indicate an objective fixity that we naturally see as repugnant to ourselves. People generally incline to see themselves and their doings not in terms of objects and their properties but in processual terms—as manifolds of teleological, agency-purposive activities geared to the satisfaction of needs and wants as they function in the circumstances of the moment. In application to ourselves, at any rate, thing-classifiers have a status mien that is naturally distasteful to us.

However, from the angle of a process metaphysic, the situation has a rather different look. We have difficulties in apprehending what we *are*, but have little difficulty in experiencing what we *do*. Our bodily and mental activities lie wide open to our experiential apprehension. There is no problem with experiential access to the processes and patterns of process that characterize us personally—our doings and undergoings, either individually or patterned into talents, skills, capabilities, traits, dispositions, habits, inclinations, and tendencies to action and inaction are, after all, what characteristically define a person as the individual he or she is. And what makes my experience mine is not some peculiar qualitative character that it exhibits, but simply its forming part of the overall ongoing process that delineates and constitutes my life. We face no insuperable obstacle in seeing ourselves defined—in processual terms—as constituted by the systemic utility of our actual and potential actions, by what we do (by our *career* to use Chisholm's own aptly chosen word).

Chisholm insists (p. 123) on seeing "feeling depressed" and

"being appeared to redly" as *properties* (i.e., nonrelational qualities) of a person. But why not see "going through a period of depression" or "experiencing an appearance of red" as processes—in particular, as subprocesses that constitute part of the macroprocess that constitutes a person? What legislates that we must see such items as descriptive *properties of substances* rather than—surely more naturally—as *components of processes*?

If we take a person's identity to inhere (wholly or primarily) in physical (bodily) continuity, then we encounter all of those gradual replacement problems dear to philosophers (not to speak of the brain transplantation envisioned by science fiction writers), and that are reflected in Chisholm's concern with the shape of the setting and its difficulties. But, if we see a person's identity in terms of a processual unity—as a macroprocess constituted through a mutually integrated system of component subprocesses—then many of these difficulties can be averted.

Once we conceptualize the core "self" of a person as a unified manifold of actual and potential process—of action and capacities, tendencies, and dispositions to action (both physical and psychical)—then we have a concept of personhood that renders the self or ego experientially accessible, seeing that experiencing itself simply *consists* of such processes. On a process-oriented approach, the self or ego (the constituting core of a person as such, that is, as the particular person he-or-she is) simply a megaprocess—a *structured system of processes*, a cohesive and (relatively) stable center of agency. The unity of person is a unity of experience—the coalescence of all of one's diverse microexperience as part of one unified macroprocess. (It is the same sort of unity of process that links each minute's level into a single overall journey.) The crux—and principle attraction—of this approach is its shift in orientation from substance to process—from a unity of hardware, of physical machinery, to a unity of software, of programming or mode of functioning.

Miguel de Unamuno asserted that Descartes got it backwards—that instead of *cogito, ergo sum res cogitans* it should be: *sum res cogitans, ergo cogito*.[9] But this is not so. Descartes' reversal of Scholasticism's traditional substance-prioritizing is perfectly in order, based on the sound idea that activity comes first ("*Im Anfang war die Tat*")—that what we do defines what we are. The fundamentality of psychic process for the constitution of a self was put on the agenda of modern philosophy by

Descartes, even though he himself remained deeply enmeshed in the work of the theory paradigm.[10]

The salient advantage of a view of the self as an internally complex process of "leading a life (of a particular sort)"—with its natural division into a varied manifold of constituent sub-processes—is that it does away with the need for a mysterious and experientially inaccessible unifying substantial *entity* (on the lines of Kant's "transcendental ego") to constitute a self out of the variety of its experiences. The unity of self comes to be seen as a unity of process—of one large, integrated megaprocess that encompasses many smaller ones in its makeup. Such an approach wholly rejects the thing-ontologist's view of a person as an *entity* existing separately from its actions, activities, and experiences. We arrive at a view of mind that dispenses with the Cartesian "ghost in the machine" and looks to the unity of mind as a unity of functioning—of *operation* rather than *operator*. A "self" is viewed not as a *thing* but as a unified though internally complex process.

On this basis, the Humean complaint—"One experiences feeling this and doing that, but one never experiences *one-self*"—is much like the complaint of the person who says "I see him picking up that brick, and mixing that batch of mortar, and cementing that brick into place, but I never see him building a wall." Even as "building the wall" just exactly *is* the complex process that is *composed* of those various activities, so—from the process point of view—one's self just *is* this complex process *composed* of those various physical and psychic experiences, actions, and responses taken as subprocesses in their systemic interrelationship within one overarching superprocess. The process-based approach in philosophical psychology doubtless has difficulties of its own. But there is no good reason to think that they decisively outweigh those of the traditional substantival approach.

There yet remains Chisholm's charge that process philosophers have expended insufficient philosophical toil. Touché. There is much justice in this charge. Yet, all the same, it seems to be true—universally and invariantly—that a philosophical position is never developed as fully as its opponents would require. For, of course, these opponents standardly see the position as replete with difficulties and defects—real or imagined—which, to *their* mind, its proponents have not resolved satisfactorily. Chisholm is no doubt right that process philosophy stands in need of further development. But what philosophical position—traditionalistic substance/attribute metaphysics included—is exempt from this stricture? In philosophy there is always more to be done.

And, in any case, is the situation that obtains here really as bad as Chisholm suggests? Perhaps it is true that ordinary language favors the grammar of object and property over that of subject and verbs—though there is room for doubt here. But matters surely stand otherwise with the machinery of differential equations, the language of process. In this regard as in so many others, Leibniz had insight far beyond his time. Important though subject-predicate discourse may be (and he stresses that they are *very* important), it is the *mathematical* language of process—of transformation functions and differential equations—that process philosophers from Leibniz to Whitehead—both of them first-rate mathematicians—have always emphasized.

To be sure, if Chisholm were right and insurmountable difficulties ensured for a process approach at the level of something as fundamental as logic and semantics, then the substance ontologists would be within sight of an easy victory. But the present deliberations suggest that no such facile triumph is available to them, the process approach affording an available option to a far greater extent than Chisholm's treatment of the issue would lead his readers to suspect. Chisholm's metaphysical deliberations exaggerate the merits of a traditionalistic ontology of things. A case can be made out for the claim that there is more vitality and more promise to process ontology than is dreamt of in Roderick Chisholm's ingenious philosophy.

Notes

1. Unless explicitly noted to the contrary, all references to Chisholm's discussions are to his *On Metaphysics* (Minneapolis: University of Minnesota Press, 1989).

2. See the essay "Exits from Paradox" in the author's *Satisfying Reason* (Dordrecht: Reidel, 1994).

3. See George J. Klir and Tina A. Folger, *Fuzzy Sets, Uncertainty, and Information* (Prentice Hall: Englewood Cliffs, NJ, 1988).

4. See the author's *Many-Valued Logic* (New York: McGraw Hill, 1969; reprinted Godstone, UK: Gregg Revivals, 1994).

5. "Identity Through Time" in *On Metaphysics, op. cit.*, pp. 25-41.

6. Chisholm himself views with favor (p. 123) G. T. Fechner's double-aspect theory that while intrinsically, "to ourselves" persons are psychical, extrinsically "for others" they are material (physical). But it is all too clear that others always constitute an overwhelming majority.

7. David Hume, *A Treatise of Human Nature*, bk. I, pt. iv, sec. 6, "Of Personal Identity." In the Appendix, Hume further elaborates: "When I turn my reflection on *myself*, I never can perceive this *self* without some one or more perceptions; nor can I ever perceive anything but the [sensory] perceptions. It is the composition of these, therefore, which forms the SELF."

8. J. P. Sartre, "Bad Faith" in *Being and Nothingness*, tr. by Hazel Barnes (Pocket Book edition, New York: Washington Square Press, 1966), pp. 107F.

9. Miguel de Unamuno, *Del sentimiento trágico de la vida*, ed. by P. Felix Garcia (Madrid: Espasa-Calpe, 1982), p. 52.

10. On this theme see Gilbert Ryle's *Concept of Mind* (London: Hutchinson, 1949).

Chapter Ten

RELIGIOUS BELIEF AND SCIENTIFIC METHOD

1. THE PROBLEM

THIS discussion will deliberate about the evidential support that the observed character of the world can provide for faith in God. Its central concern is with the prospects of warrantedly inferring theistic positions and doctrines from our observation of the world's facts. Its focal issue is that of the extent to which it makes sense to expect support for theology in science's teachings regarding nature.

Let us begin by contemplating two somewhat extreme alternatives in this regard. On the one hand, consider first a god whose impact on the world's nature and events is so clear and decisive as to put his existence and operations effectively beyond the doubt of that world's inhabitants. Recall in this context one of the most vivid episodes in the Old Testament, the story of the comeuppance of the prophets of Baal at the hands of the prophet Elijah (I Kings 18-20):

> Elijah said unto the prophets of Baal, Choose you one bullock for yourselves, and dress it first; for ye are many; and call on the name of your gods, but put no fire under. And they took the bullock which was given them, and they dressed it, and called on the name of Baal from morning even until noon, saying, O Baal, hear us. But there was no voice, nor any that answered. And they danced upon the altar which was made. And it came to pass at noon, that Elijah mocked them, and said, Cry aloud: for he is a god; either he is talking, or he is hunting, or he is on a journey, or peradventure he sleepeth, and must be awaked...[Then Elijah] built an altar in the name of the LORD: and he made a trench about the altar, as great as would contain two measures of seed. And he put the wood in order, and cut the bullock in pieces, and laid him on the wood, and said, Fill four barrels with water, and pour it on the burnt sacrifice, and

on the wood. And he said, Do it the second time. And they did it the second time. And he said, Do it the third time. And they did it the third time. And the water ran round about the altar; and he filled the trench also with water...[Then Elijah] said, LORD God of Abraham, Isaac, and of Israel, let it be known this day that thou art God in Israel, and that I am thy servant, and that I have done all these things at thy word. Hear me, O LORD, hear me, that this people may know that thou art the LORD God, and that thou hast turned their heart back again. Then the fire of the LORD fell, and consumed the burnt sacrifice, and the wood, and the stones, and the dust, and licked up the water that was in the trench. And when all the people saw it, they fell on their faces: and they said, The LORD, he is the God; the LORD, he is the God.

We have here a word-picture that Cecil B. deMille himself could hardly render more dramatic on celluloid, affording a vivid illustration of a possibility for God's virtually uncontestable action upon the stage of the world's causal commerce. The only thing that gives one slight unease about the evidential capacity of the episode to engender absolute conviction among believers is the marked reluctance of Elijah's successors among the priests and prophets of Jehovah to offer to repeat the experiment.

Now by contrast consider, ever so much more prosaically, the hypothesis of a world whose observed makeup is intrinsically of such a nature as to throw deep doubt upon the idea that it can be the handiwork of a benevolent being—a world of utter chaos and confusion, of arrant brutality, injustice, and unfairness, where the ungodly thrive, and where it is all too frequently from the lips of hypocrites that we hear the name of God.

To all appearances, the real world about us is far closer to the second extreme than to the first. But it should be stressed that even if the second prospect were realized yet more drastically than is actually the case, this fact alone would not speak decisively for atheism. The perhaps unwelcome truth is that the question "On the general principles of the matter, what sorts of observable signs of his questions could God be expected to make available?" is by no means a simple one to resolve. For not only are negatives notoriously harder to establish than positives, but it is possible to imagine all sorts of cogent reasons why even a benign God might be responsible for the existence of an awful world. (The *Theodicy* of Leibniz provides an arsenal of supportive argumentation here.) And in the final analysis, there is no good theoretical reason for supposing that God should be a noisy intruder on the world's stage rather than a hidden God who invites belief while yet remaining comparatively inconspicuous in his (or her) dealings with free agents. After all, look at the issue from God's own point of view. Surely the only believers worth having are those whose hand is unforced and who are motivated by inner conviction.

In principle, then, it would seem that while it is indeed possible for the observed facts of science and of history to speak convincingly for theism, this is not something we are entitled to expect. And so, the question remains, to what extent is this theoretical prospect realized. Does the observed nature of our universe evidentiate God?

2. God and Scientific Method

From Old Testament times onwards, philosophizing theology has never lacked for people who want to argue for God on scientific principles through inference to the best explanation from the observed character of the real. This tradition of natural theology attained one of its high-water marks in England in the seventeenth and eighteenth centuries. Already the great Sir Isaac Newton— urged on by Samuel Clarke, Richard Bentley, and others—represented his theory of the solar system as confirming in its need for a stabilizing influence the helpful interaction of a benign deity in nature's scheme of things. And from the time of Newton until that of Darwin, Anglican theology took a decidedly naturalistic turn.

This line of development for "natural religion" (as it came to be called) did not, however, constitute an auspicious precedent. Laplace's demonstration of the earth's orbital stability expelled Newton's clockmaker God from the solar system and shifted the center of gravity of natural theology from astronomy to biology—from God as designer of the celestial order to God as contriver of the organic domain. And then—alas—Darwin came along. His theory of evolution by natural selection expelled Louis Agassiz's contriver God from the realm of biology as well. T. H. Huxley and his eager supporters gave theo-teleological biology some hard knocks. The destructive impact of modern science on Anglican natural theology does not auger auspiciously for the promise of such an enterprise.

To be sure, natural theology is making a major comeback in our day. Recent years have seen the paving of a new and influential pathway between science and theism, based on the quantum-theoretic cosmology. In the wake of the big bang theory of physical cosmology, an analysis of the quantum theoretic processes that govern the first mini-instants of cosmic evolution affords some suggestive data for the natural theologian. For it indicates that an incredibly elaborate fine-tuning was necessary to adjust the cosmic constants in the first microseconds of post-big-bang cosmic history in such a way that the resultant universe could in due course provide a stage suitable for the evolution of intelligent life. The leading idea of the anthropic principle is, roughly, that the physical universe had to be just about exactly the way it is for intelligent life to be able to develop in it.[1] In short, we are to envision a universe congenial to the development of creatures such as ourselves.

From this essentially scientific hypothesis it is but a short step to a theological glossing of the situation.[2] For on its basis, various scientist-theologians have projected the anthropic hypothesis of an intelligence-friendly universe that should—how could it be otherwise?—be seen as the handiwork of an intelligence-friendly creative intelligence. The idea is, roughly, that God's workmanship is manifest in nature through the fact that nature favors intelligent beings because its laws are such that (1) only a very peculiar and idiosyncratic set of parametric conditions could have permitted the development of beings of our kind, and (2) it seems difficult to suppose that it was simply by chance that the primal condition of the universe "just happened" to realize these extraordinary and inherently unlikely conditions. On this basis, God is brought upon the stage of natural science as part of the theoretical mechanism of inference to the best explanation because theism—so it is maintained—affords our best explanation of the anthropic principle. Here explanatory reasoning based on observational experience comes round in a full circle to the program of traditional natural theology with God not just in his heaven but down here in the technical institutes helping our scientists out in their explanatory work.

The trouble with the anthropic theologian's reasoning that the universe is constituted as it is *in order to* produce (human) life is that it rests on the idea that if the universe were substantially different, then life would not have emerged. And the difficulty with this is that it involves the tacit rider that life would then not have emerged *on the prevailing principles of natural law*. But, of course, that life's emergence in the world should be intricately and indissolubly linked to the details of this world's particular operating principles is, in the final analysis, something that is only to be expected. Perhaps it is surprising that a world exists at all—that there is something rather than nothing.[3] But once a world exists in the particular fashion at issue, then the fact that it should have some particular feature—such as containing long-necked or sapient beings—can no longer be seen as something so extraordinary as to require further explanation in extra- or supranatural terms.[4] Natural law and accidental chance between them provide enough machinery to handle the explanatory job.

Be all this as it may, the fact remains that, its ingenuity and impressive scientific credentials notwithstanding, the anthropic argument represents a high-risk strategy for theistic argumentation. The manifest dangers of this strategy were already clearly foreshadowed in the dramaturgy of the Laplace-to-Darwin period. The God who is invoked to help the scientists of one era out of their exploratory difficulties—the God of the gaps—is too easily given his walking papers when later scientists manage to find other expedients for accomplishing the job. If we look for God with the lens of a microscope or telescope, then we may well in the end achieve no more than to discern ever vaster reaches of matter and physical process whose character is emphatically natural rather than divine.

As far as the world-picture of contemporary natural science goes, we live in a world shaped and pervaded by contingency. Each of us is here, and our whole species is here—and our planet and our galaxy—as the result of an unfathomably large proliferation of accidents. And this situation is profoundly ambiguous. One can read it as meaning that chance governs all—that natural history is one great crap-shoot. Or one can see the hand of God moving invisibly through the interstices of chance. Nothing decisively constrains our judgment either way. Every reason that theologians can offer to explain why prophets-of-Baal-type episodes are not daily commonplaces provides a reason why God is invisible in nature too.

3. GOD AND NON-OBSERVATIONAL EXPERIENCE

The inherent problems and difficulties which, over the years, people have been encountered in supporting theism by inference from *observational* experience have led some religious theoreticians and theologians to contemplate a turn to

nonobservational experience. When thus relying on nonobservational experience to support religious belief, the theological tradition of the West has looked to the role of people of a
special sensibility, people who function as it were as special
receptors of communications from God. These special messengers have come to be known under the name of *prophets*. In all
three of the major monotheistic religions of the West they have
played a special and prominent part.

A. Prophecy

From the cognitive point of view, the principal difficulty
with prophecy lies in the area of authentication. There are basically two ways to authenticate prophecies, namely by the content of the message and by the credentials of the messenger.
Each has its problems from the probative point of view.

Note, to begin with, that when we authenticate prophecies
by the *content* of the message, then we must, clearly, already
regard this content as valid and appropriate. And this means
that in some substantial degree those content-validated messages have to be redundant with preexisting, already validated
beliefs. They are, as it were, yesterday's news. And this circumstance clearly limits their theological usefulness and efficacy.

A variant approach accordingly seems in order, and it is generally provided by the very different procedure of validating
the prophetic message not so much through its content as
through the credentials of the messenger. Exactly this was
clearly the situation *vis-à-vis* the prophets of Baal in the dramatic Elijah episode mentioned earlier on. But for better or for
worse, messengers who work such overwhelmingly convincing miracles are, to put it mildly, few and far between. Moreover, they have the unfortunate tendency to operate in times
and places where we ourselves are not, so that we are linked to
them only through a chain of generally more or less problematic witnesses. And so the New Testament contemplates—
against the background of the Elijah authentication—what is a
somewhat less demanding but still impressive standard. As the
ending of St. Mark's gospel puts it:

> Afterward he [Jesus] appeared unto the eleven as they sat at
> meal, and upbraided them with their unbelief and hardness of
> heart, because they believed not them which had seen him af-
> ter he was risen. And he said unto them, Go ye into all the
> world, and preach the gospel to every creature...And these

signs shall accompany them that [truly] believe; In my name shall they cast out devils; they shall speak [intelligibly] with new tongues. They shall take up serpents; and if they drink any deadly thing, it shall not hurt them; they shall lay hands on the sick, and they shall recover.

Authentication here is a matter not of working *miracles* but merely of doing *wonders*. But even this sort of thing is pretty unusual. The gospel ministry would be far less audible than it is if the way to the microphone were paved with boa constrictors. Rare is the would-be spokesmen for Christ—Rasputin perhaps apart—who is prepared to volunteer for the strychnine test. It is little wonder that few men are acknowledged as prophets in their own country—and even abroad prophets have their problems.

B. Mystical Experience

There is, however, yet another prospect—a sort of experiential halfway house which, like prophetical experience, is indeed somewhat unusual but which, like observational experience, is in principle available to all. The issue here is that of *mystical* experience which, in its highest and most developed forms, is the resource of masters of spirituality, but which in a more modest way, is at the disposal of virtually all practitioners of prayer and meditation. The mystics constitute a cloud of witnesses whose testimony is extensive and impressive.

The difficulty here is in determining exactly what to make of this sort of thing. The problem lies in making sense of the mystics' deliverances when they talk with the rest of us. The substance of religious experience is clearly not all that easily conveyed in everyday language. And the one thing that mystics of every kind and affiliation are agreed on is the inability of the language of ordinary communication to provide an adequate vehicle for the description of their experiences. Accordingly, mystical experience too is an evidential resource of limited capabilities.

4. GOD AND DEMONSTRATION

In the end, then, we have to face the fact that none of the strictly experiential pathways to God is altogether free from problems and difficulties. Each confronts certain epistemic obstacles. After all, experience (of any sort) cannot exert more weight than the mind of the experiencer can bear, and the human mind is a frail and imperfect instrument. Perhaps, then, we had best rest the case for theism on a different, extra-experiential basis.

This line of thought has led philosophically minded theologians in virtually every era to turn from experience to reason, and to move away not only from observation but from experience in general to take recourse to some sort of reasoning and reflection unassisted by experience in an endeavor to ground belief in the sphere of the demonstrative. This tendency produced, time and again, a shift from concrete experience to abstract reason.

From the viewpoint of theorists of this inclination, the ideal course would be one of settling the question of God's nature and existence on the basis of general principles of theoretical reflection. The aim and aspiration is to validate belief by rational argumentation from the very nature of concepts and the communicative mechanisms at our disposal for handling them ("*ex vi terminorum*").

At this stage we come to the tradition of St. Anselm of Canterbury with his Ontological Argument and St. Thomas Aquinas with his Five Ways. A tendency of thought comes to expression here that has always appealed to logically oriented minds. Even Bertrand Russell when young and ardent–before his ideological arteries had hardened into scientism–indulged some fancies in this direction. In his essay on "My Mental Development," Russell records:

> I remember the precise moment, one day in 1894, as I was walking along Trinity Lane [in Cambridge], when I saw in a flash (or thought I saw) that the ontological argument is valid. I had gone out to buy a tin of tobacco; on my way back, I suddenly threw it up in the air, and exclaimed as I caught it: "Great Scott, the ontological argument is sound."[5]

The example of Russell clearly instantiates David Hume's sly observation that the ontological argument exerts a special appeal for mathematically inclined intellects "who have accustomed themselves to abstract reasoning."[6]

However, as the development of the philosophical tradition shows, this abstract reason-based approach to the validation of a belief in God also has its problems. Some of them arise on theological, and especially apologetic, grounds. That they do not suit all conditions of men is clearly indicated by Miguel de

Unamuno's acid dictum that the scholastic proofs serve principally in the production of atheists.[7] Other objections proceed on grounds of theoretical general principle. After all, there are, in theory, four possible positions regarding the inferential relationship between the world's observed character and the existence of a benign and intelligent creator/arranger according as one maintains that the two are

1. inferentially disconnected

2. inferentially connected

   (2.1) in a positive, theism favoring way

   (2.2) in a negative, theism counterindicating way

   (2.3) in an imponderable and evidentially inconclusive way

Here my own position favors that last alternative. After all, the rational linkage between evidence and conclusion is always a matter of a conditional *inference*—of what is in principle a complex sort of calculation under the aegis of arithmetically mathematicizable rules. And the fact is that the issue of God's existence and modus operandi is something too complex for the limited resources of arithmetical calculation. (Indeed, as Gödel has shown even mathematics itself is too complex to be caught in our reason's net of recursive formalization.)[8]

5. Pascal's Turning

There is, moreover, yet another, *anthropologically* based objection to rationalizing theology that perhaps no one has articulated more eloquently than Blaise Pascal. Pascal articulates a profound theological discontent with the reliance on abstract reasonings in this context. He questions whether the God whom theologians find at the end of a syllogism is the sort of being in whom one can possibly recognize the God of Israel and the God of Jesus—the God of our fathers and of our fears and hopes and deepest affections. Pascal like many others—and perhaps in the end even St. Thomas Aquinas himself—could not quite bring himself to regard the God of an abstract theoretical proof as a deity to whom one can worship—and who relates to us as a loving father of whom one can ask aid and mercy and to whom one can pray for strength and spiritual sustenance.

Somewhat paradoxically, the person who is authentically religious within the monotheistic tradition of the West is both

God-loving and God-fearing. And when we love and fear, we do so partly for *reasons* but also partly because of *motives* that are inherent in our natures and dispositions. Love in particular roots in our affinities and affective attachments—we love not because we are rationally "well advised" to do so but because, in the circumstances we simply must. We love our God as we love our parents or wives or children—not so much because they are, factually speaking, the most deserving of persons, but simply because we are parts of one another. The sort of God whom one finds at the termination of a syllogism or of a course of scientific reasoning is not the sort of God who can do the whole of the job that needs to be done in the context of authentic religion.

Against this background, Pascal proposed an overtly anthropological line of departure. He espoused the approach of grounding faith in a palpably realistic aspect of the human situation. Specifically, his idea was that, given the actualities of the human situation, we are well advised not to look for evidence of God "out there" in factors external to ourselves—in observations, experiences, inferences, and demonstrations. Rather we should do well to ground our faith inwardly, in the sphere of our inner nature and its needs—in the yearnings of our heart.

The argumentation at issue in Pascal's thinking contemplates various practical/pragmatic lines of thought that support faith in God:

— Without God, life is meaningless/empty

— We cannot (should not) accept that life is meaningless/empty

— We cannot (should not) believe there is no God

And again:

— Without God, the world is ultimately unintelligible

— We cannot (should not) accept that the world is ultimately unintelligible

— We cannot (should not) believe there is no God

Such arguments do not establish the existence of God as a *factual* but rather as a *practical* conclusion—one whose acceptability rests on other than evidential grounds. Accordingly strictly cognitive considerations are not the pivotal point at all, it is our human feelings that lie at the crux. (As Pascal viewed the matter, the heart too has "reasons" of its own of which our Reason as such knows nothing.)

On this basis, Pascal proceeded to endorse an appeal to experience of sorts. But not cognitive or evidential experience. Rather, he saw the issue as turning on the experience of actually living the religious life—of finding that belief can follow in the wake of lifestyle, that a life of committed religious praxis gradually brings a clarity of mind in its wake. As Pascal saw it, the emotional and spiritual ("heart"-oriented) benefits of the religious life carry conviction. And they do so in that we come to recognize through them the answers not so much to our *questions* as to our *needs*. If we try the life of faith—so Pascal insists —then we will come to recognize in it the solution of problems —not problems of *mind* but problems of heart and spirit.

But of course Pascal's reflections too have their problematic aspect. A certain element of wishful thinking broods over his probative proceedings. His theology looks to an experiential engagement in religious practice—a strategy whose persuasive impetus fails to content more rationalistically inclined theoreticians.

6. A COMMON DESTINATION OF MANY PATHS

It is time to pause and take stock. In these brief deliberations we have surveyed a wide spectrum of probative approaches in theology, approaches looking to such different factors as:

- observational evidence

- inner experience (be it affective or spiritual)

- explanatory systematization

- conceptually geared inference or demonstration

On every side we have found both pluses and minuses—both promises and problems. What, then, is one to make of such a diversified manifold of very different probative approaches, each with its own points of appeal and its own difficulties, its assets and liabilities? Is the result simply a confusion where the different elements cancel one another out? Is the *isostheneia* of the ancient sceptics perhaps the best and most appropriate reading of the situation here?

It is deeply implausible to suppose that this is so. For such a reaction would be a profoundly inadequate construction of the actual state of affairs. The sensible view of the situation is that these different approaches are not mutually annihilative but

164 / PHILOSOPHICAL STUDIES

mutually reinforcing. For these reasonings manifest a consilience, a systemic coordination in the manner illustrative of the
classical coherence epistemology. Each takes its place in a comprehensive mosaic of theological reflection. They represent not
a chain that is no stronger than its weakest link, but a rope with
various mutually reinforcing threads. Each makes its modest
and imperfect contribution to a complex and many-sided
whole. Each fails to be definitively decisive in and by itself, but
none is totally ineffective either. And the whole complex should
be seen not as rival and mutually destructive approaches, but as
elements of a diversified fabric of thought that bears impressive
witness to the human spirit's commitment and entitlement to
belief in a God-governed reality.

And this surely is how it *ought* to be. The world, after all,
contains very different sorts of people with very different sorts
of needs, inclinations, interests, capacities, and the like. Accordingly, religious faith and belief at large requires not just one
kind of appeal fitted to one kind of mind, but a diversified plurality of supports attuned to the differing dispositions of various
different sorts of minds. What theology all too obviously needs
is a complex epistemology for a complex world. A God interested in reaching people so as to call them to himself must be a
God who, as a destination, admits different avenues of access.

From this perspective, the phenomenon of a plurality of diverse and even discordant approaches to the evidentiation of
faith itself constitutes a theologically significant consideration.
Each line of thought exerts an influence on people of a certain
cast of mind and fails with respect to others. And this circumstance clearly reflects the internal diversity and complexity of
religion's constituency as a plurality composed of many different sorts of people who have to be reached in many different
sorts of ways. Human nature and human circumstances are
multi-faceted and prismatic, reflecting the diversified complexity of the situation of *Homo sapiens* here on earth. People do
not display simply one single kind of mentality with one single
kind of sensibility. And not only do we encounter diversification and differentiation with different people, but even with
the phases and stages of a single individual. The youth has a
sensibility different from that of the senior citizen, the sheep
herder one that differs from that of the urban policeman. We
see matters differently on days when all goes well than on days
of darkness, at the times of calm than at times of trouble. Condi-

tions make a difference: different sorts of appeals make a different impact upon us at different stages and seasons.

The evidentiation of faith accordingly cannot—and should not—be seen as a single-solution issue. For no one single resolution can possibly be adequate to the variable needs of the situation. The fact that St. Thomas Aquinas offered us not one but five ways to show the existence of God is deeply symbolic. The problem of faith can have a single solution no more than can the problem of life. We can no more relate to our God in one single monochromatic mode than we can so relate to those we love here on earth. It seems only plausible that there should be different pathways to God suited to the condition of different sorts of people. One monolithic theology can fit the diversity of human dispositions no more than one size of shoe will fit all human feet.[10]

The fact of variation—of a spectrum of alternatives—is not without evidential relevancy. The existence of so many different paths to a common destination is itself an evidential factor in support of faith. It represents a consilience not of *inductions* but of *reflections*, betokening at once the pervasive need of *Homo sapiens* for contact with a transcendent being and reality's forthcomingness in responding to such a need through an ample arsenal of justifying considerations. The very diversity at issue itself betokens the prospect of a divine outreach towards diversely constituted people.

7. THE LIMITED SCOPE OF SCIENCE: ITS UNCONCERN FOR THE VALUE DIMENSION

The preceding deliberations have insisted that the "scientific" approach to theism in terms of inference to the best explanatory systematization of observational experience is only one among others—one item of limited utility within a box of various different tools suited to the cast of mind of diversely constituted individuals. Thus even if one acknowledges the potential effectiveness of this "scientific" approach—and accepts the plausibility of seeking for a hallmark of God's workmanship in the world we see as the product of his creation—it should also be stressed that this should not be given a central place of paramount importance.[11]

Let us now consider more closely just why it is that one should not rely on this "scientific" approach to belief more extensively—why we should not put all our eggs into the basket of "the God hypothesis" viewed naively as part and parcel of an inference to the best explanation of the world's observable phenomena, in the manner of the argument from design or of the anthropic cosmogony.

The fact is that the epistemology of science is only one among others. We humans, after all, are not just subject to the *intellectual* mode of knowledge but also to the *affective*. For us, there is not only observational experience but evaluational experience as well. And with its focus on observation science ignores the reactive, affective, and person-linked dimension of human cognition: sympathy, empathy, feeling, insight, and evaluation.[12] Value-appreciation—how things strike people within the affective setting of their personal (and perhaps idiosyncratic) experiences or their sociocultural (group-conditioned) background—is something science deliberately leaves aside in its dedication to the impersonally observable features of things.

Accordingly, science omits from its register of what is worth taking at face value the whole affective, emotional, feeling-oriented side of our cognitive life. Scientific understanding does not of itself teach us to enjoy and appreciate the cornucopia of our life's eventuation.

Consider just one example. Thanks to its prescinding from normative and evaluative concerns in the pursuit of its strictly cognitive mission, science approaches people as objects of study, as *things*, and not as *persons*. The sort of "knowledge" of a person in which it trades is not that of a friend or companion, based on concern inherent in mutual interaction, but the detached, "impersonal" knowledge of a doctor, biologist, or sociologist—the knowledge of observation rather than communion. The aspects of mutual recognition and interrelated reciprocity are lost; and such cognitive modes as sympathy and empathy are put aside. The cognitive approach of science to man's understanding of man deliberately puts aside that element of recognition as a fellow man characteristic of all genuinely human relationships among people. (To be sure, to speak of *conflict* here would be to succumb to a confusion between diverse perspectives of consideration—between different levels of concern and inquiry. Science is not *opposed* to these concerns, it is *irrelevant* to them; it simply ignores them, having other fish to fry. The scientific mode of understanding takes the externalized route of causal explanation, and not the internalized route of affective interpretation and personal interrelationships.[13])

And so, insofar as our relationship to God is a matter of a personal relationship with a potency that gives comfort and meaning to human existence in the world of nature, science as such has no particular concern with the matter. Accordingly, in seeking for probative support of revelation we are surely better advised to look elsewhere–to looking within the human domain–to tradition, revelation, inward experience in meditation and prayer, and to a thoughtful reflection on the nature of the human condition as we and our fellows experience it–rather than to looking without, to the observationally detectable feature of the world's physical machinations. (It is not from science that we do–or can–learn to see other humans as units of dignity and worth–not merely members of *Homo sapiens* but *persons* who are to be treated as ends but not means, with a value equal to one's own in the sight of God.)

Ludwig Wittgenstein wrote:

> We feel that even if *all possible* scientific questions be answered, the problems of life have still not been touched at all. Of course there is then no question left, and just this is the answer.[14]

Wittgenstein is right in this–that the salient problems of life and spirit are still left unresolved when science has had its say. But he is profoundly and perversely wrong in thinking that there is no remainder–no questions left. For this perversely austere perspective pivots on the deeply problematic view that scientific issues are the only ones there are–that where no scientific question is at issue, nothing remains to be said, and that factual information is the end of the cognitive line. If this position is adopted, then questions relating to normative and evaluative issues of significance, meaning, and validity–questions relative to beauty or duty or justice, for example–can all be set at naught. Such a response does indeed resolve the "problems of life," but only by casting them away into the outer darkness. But nothing within or about science demands such a dehumanization of our sensibilities. To take this stance is not to celebrate science but to distort it–to see it as prejudging and prejudicing matters that lie outside the scope of its definitive mission as a cognitive enterprise. It is to move from science to scientism, from science as inquiry to science as ideology.

8. Science Is of Limited Theological Utility

The fact is that, as an inherently purposive endeavor, science has a determinate mission of its own in regard to prediction, evaluation and control with respect to the phenomena of nature. And here, as elsewhere, determination is negation, and since science is a certain definite kind of enterprise, there are also various things that science is not. And theology is one of them.[15] People who maintain that science is the be-all and end-all—that what is not in science textbooks is not worth knowing—are not unusually rigorous and sophisticated thinkers but ideologists with a peculiar and distorted doctrine of their own. For them, science is no longer a sector of the cognitive enterprise but an all-inclusive world-view. And this, clearly, is the doctrine not of *science* but of *scientism*; to take this stance is not to celebrate science but to distort it by casting the mantle of its authority over issues it was not designed to address as components of its characterizing problem mandate. Even among the "modes of knowledge," science represents only one among others. It is geared to the use of theory to triangulate from objectively observational experience to answer our questions about how things work in the world. But there are many other areas in which we have a reflective interest—areas wholly outside the province of science.

Homo sapiens is a member not just of the *intellectual* but also of the specifically *affective and evaluative* order of things, and correspondingly there is knowledge of the brain and knowledge of the heart. And science as we know it—as it has in actual fact evolved over the centuries—simply does not address matters of this sort. This limitation is clearly no defect—any more than it is a defect that woodworking does not produce metal objects. But it is a domain limitation and as such means that there is more to reality than natural science contemplates; in the harsh but stimulating school of life, we are set examinations involving problems for whose resolution our science courses by themselves do not equip us.

We are thus led back to the main issue. There is, of course, no harm in exploring the prospects of a strictly scientific approach to theism via a strategy of inference to the best explanatory systematization of observation. Such an approach may well yield instructive insights that are, in their way, interesting and suggestive. But a crucial caution is in order. Those who rest their religious convictions on the data of science take a position that stands or falls by the indications of those data. And if historical experience has taught us any one thing, it is that science is changeable. The scientific truths of today all too easily prove to be the scientific errors of tomorrow. The luminiferous ether has long ago gone the way of philogiston. One scientist's cold fusion is another's overheated delusion. The massive merits of natural science notwithstanding, those who base their philosophy (or theology or ideology) on the teachings of the science of the day do not really have all that solid a foundation.

Moreover, we do well to bear in mind that the scientific approach to human experience—whatever be its strengths and weaknesses—can make good no claim to exclusivity. Even at best and under the most favorable of suppositions, it is no more than one approach among others—an approach which speaks to one particular set of interests and concerns characterizing the human situation. The observed nature of the world—be it the world of nature or that of human behavior—has only such a remote and complicated bearing on the substantive issues of religious belief that it would be unwise indeed to put all one's eggs into this basket, and to look here for a mainstay support of theological teachings. For better or for worse, science has its limits from the theological point of view. It seems only sensible to take the position that the impact of the divine in this world is less likely to make itself felt in connection with material nature than in the region of the mind and spirit of intelligent beings.

The nineteenth-century vision of a *warfare* between science and religion deserves being abandoned. For what is at issue is not a struggle where one party must ultimately end up as *subordinate* to the other, but a division of labor where each is *coordinate* with the other. Each has a different problem-agenda; each deals with a different dimension of human concerns and a different section of human experience. To be sure, they are not altogether disconnected (human experience is one and its different sections have to coexist and coordinate). But they are sufficiently different that the amount of intellectual converse between them is bound to be small, and that neither is in a position to do the other substantial harm (or benefit).

Ultimately the issue is one of legitimation. If you think that science is the sole depository of intellectual rigor and cogency, then it is there that you must place your religious bets as well. (And good luck to you, because you'll need it!) But if you are prepared to trust not only your heart but your intellectual appreciation of the human condition as based in the shared experience of yourself and your fellows—construed comprehensively to include affective experience as well as observation experience—then matters take on a different aspect.

9. A METHODOLOGICAL CODA

Some concluding words of caution regarding the purport of these deliberations are in order. First this. Religion is certainly not a matter of affective and evaluative considerations alone; it clearly has a cognitive component based on convictions and beliefs. But, for many or most believers at any rate, the *probative backing* of these beliefs will not and cannot be a matter of science-reminiscent inferential reasoning from mere observations, personal or vicarious. ("Blessed are they that have not seen, and yet have believed," John 20:29.) Insofar as *evidence* and *reasoning* enter into it, it is geared less to inference based on sensory information about the world's occurrences than to our experience of their meaning or "significance" in the widest sense of that term. What matters most here is an overall harmonization not just with the world's observed facts but also with our human appraisal of life's normative dimension—and so, not with what makes observation intelligible to the information-seeking side of our intellect, but with what makes human experience meaningful to the evaluative side of our intellect.

Secondly, another caution. Modern liberal theology often construes religious contentions as something fundamentally different from factual assertions—as expressing feelings, conveying moral injunctions, evincing an existential orientation towards one's context, etc. But this is emphatically not the sort of line that is adopted here. Rather, what is at issue here is a position that takes these sorts of things (feelings, moral appraisals, orientational stances, etc.) as themselves affording a body of relevant facts, and then proceeds to ask how we who possess such experiential resources can best make good rational sense of a world in which they are taken at face value. The focus is on the specifically human dimension of experience. Such a project is not different from science in its *spirit* but rather different from science in its *nature*. Science seeks to present us with *the best explanatory systematization of the* OBSERVATIONAL *data*, while the presently contemplated approach to theology sees it as a key part of the enterprise to present us with *the best interpretative ("hermeneutical") systematization of the* NORMATIVE *data*. A commitment to "the facts" is central on both sides, but the facts at issue in theology are at bottom evaluative rather than observational ones. Worth, value, and meaning are the pivot points.[16] The enterprise continues to be cognitive and rational in character—it maintains a reliance on factuality and rational cogency all right, but implements these in a direction quite different from that of science, with very different purposes in view.

On such a perspective, science neither supports theology nor clashes with it. At the level of substantive concerns, each has its own problem domain within whose boundaries it exercises a self-sufficient and independent autonomy.[17] (To say this is not—of course—to deny an overlap at the *methodological* level, where factors like intellectual honesty, persevering inquiry, rigorous thought, and the like, do and should figure prominently on the side of intellectual process.)

Insofar as these deliberations support any overall lesson it is this: even as statesmen are needed because war is something too big and too important to be left to the generals, so theologians are needed because the cogent appreciation of humanity's place in the world's scheme of things is something too big and too important to be left to the scientists.

Notes

1. For a survey of the scientific issues see John D. Barrow and Frank J. Tipler, *The Anthropic Cosmological Principle* (Oxford: Clarendon Press, 1986).

2. To be sure, the theism of such a theory may be fairly tepid. Compare Paul Davies, *The Mind of God* (New York: Simon and Schuster, 1992).

3. On this issue see the author's *The Riddle of Existence* (Lanham, MD: University Press of America, 1984).

4. For a substantially kindred critique of the anthropic argument see Mary Midgley, *Science as Salvation* (London: Routledge, 1990).

5. *The Philosophy of Bertrand Russell*, edited by P. A. Schilpp (La Salle: Open Court, 1944), pp. 3-20, quoted from p. 10.

6. "I shall venture to add an observation, that the argument *a priori* [for God's existence] has seldom been found very convincing except to people...who have accustomed themselves to abstract reasoning, and who finding from mathematics, that the understanding frequently leads to truth, through obscurity, and contrary to first appearances, have transferred the same habit of thinking to subjects where it ought not to have place." Hume, *Dialogues Concerning Natural Religion*, part IX.

7. On the positive side, a recent questionnaire study of Spanish Catholics

showed that 3% (but *only* 3%) of respondents indicated that intellectual reasons for belief play a role in their faith. See p. 8 of the Opinión section of *El País for* 13 August 1992.

8. Even St. Thomas himself did not entrust theology altogether to the resources of reason: "It was necessary for the salvation of human beings that certain truths which transcend human reason should be made known to them by divine revelation" (*Summa Theologica*, I, a.1c).

9. On the relevant issues compare the author's *Pascal's Wager* (Notre Dame: University of Notre Dame Press, 1985).

10. This point was clearly apprehended by St. Thomas.

11. The consideration of historical figures like Napoleon or F. D. Roosevelt indicate that even with humans the inference from the visible actions to the invisible reasons and motives behind them can be highly problematic.

12. Note that affective/evaluative/normative does not necessarily imply *subjective*. Matters of *taste* are one thing; matters of thoughtful *evaluation* another. The personal is not necessarily private; we share many of our capacities and resources in common.

13. To be sure, to speak of *conflict* here would be to succumb to a confusion between diverse perspectives of consideration—between different levels of thought and inquiry. Science is not *opposed* to these concerns, it is *irrelevant* to them; it simply ignores them, having other fish to fry.

14. Ludwig Wittgenstein, *Tractatus Logico-Philosphicus* (London: Routledge, 1922), sect. 6.52.

15. It must be stressed that what we confront here is something that is not a defect or a shortcoming. It is a disability imposed by the aims of the enterprise—the objectives that characterize science as the thing it is. The characteristic cognitive task of science is the *description* and *explanation* of the phenomena—the answering of our *how?* and *why?* questions about the workings of the world. Normative questions of value, significance, legitimacy, and the like are simply "beside the point" of this project. The fact that there are issues outside its domain is not a defect of natural science but an essential aspect of its nature as a particular enterprise with a mission of its own. It is no more a defect of science that it does not deal with belles-lettres than it is a defect of dentistry that it does not deal with furniture repair. It is no deficiency of a screwdriver that it does not do the work of a hammer.

16. Note that even the question of the weight of authority is an evaluative issue.

17. Many from Galileo onwards have maintained such a conception of domain diversity. It has its difficulties, but they are not insuperable. To see them as such would be to fall into the heresy that medieval scholasticism characterized as Averroism and (quite mistakenly) attributed to the great Islamic philosopher Ibn Rushd/Averroës.

Name Index

ABOUT THE AUTHOR

Nicholas Rescher was born in Germany in 1928 and came to the U.S. at the age of nine. He completed his Ph.D. at Princeton University in two years, still at the age of twenty-two, setting a record in Princeton's Philosophy Department. He is currently University Professor of Philosophy at the University of Pittsburgh where he has been since 1961, having also served as Chairman of the Department of Philosophy and as Director of the Center for Philosophy of Science. For thirty years he was editor of the *American Philosophical Quarterly* and he was also the founding editor of the *History of Philosophy Quarterly*. The author of more than sixty books in various areas of philosophy, he was elected to permanent membership in the Institut International de Philosophie in 1970 and was elected fellow of the Academie Internationale de Philosophie des Sciences in 1984. Works by Mr. Rescher have been translated into German, Spanish, French, Italian, and Japanese; he has lectured at universities in many countries, and has occupied visiting posts at various universities in North America and in Europe (including Oxford, Konstanz, and Salamanca). He has held fellowships from the J. S. Guggenhein Foundation, the Ford Foundation, and the American Philosophical Society. In 1977 its fellows elected him an honorary member of Corpus Christi College, Oxford, and in 1983 he received an Alexander von Humboldt Humanities Prize, awarded under the auspicies of the Federal Republic of Germany "in recognition of the research accomplishments of humanistic scholars of international distinction." A former president of the American Philosophical Association (Eastern Division), of the C. S. Peirce Society, and the G. W. Leibniz Society of America, Mr. Rescher is currently a member of the board of Directors of the International Federation of Philosophical Studies, an organ of UNESCO. One of the leading contemporary exponents of philosophical idealism, Mr. Rescher has been active in the rehabilitation of the coherence theory of truth and in the reconstruction of philosophical pragmatism. He has pioneered the development of inconsistency-tolerant logics and, in the philosophy of science, the exponential retardation theory of scientific progress based on the epistemological principle that knowledge increases merely with the logarithm of the increase in information. Books about Rescher's work have appeared in English, German and Italian. His contributions to philosophy have been recognized in honorary degrees from Lehigh University, Loyola University of Chicago, and the Argentina National Autonomous University of Córdoba.

Made in the USA
Middletown, DE
05 April 2017